DISCOVER DUBLI

CONTENTS

Published for WHSmith by Thomas Cook Publishing
The Thomas Cook Group Ltd
PO Box 227, Thorpe Wood
Peterborough PE3 6PU
United Kingdom

Telephone: 01733 503571
E–mail: books@thomascook.com

Text: © The Thomas Cook Group Ltd 1999
Maps: © ERA-Maptec

ISBN 1 841570 13 3

Thomas Cook Publishing
Publisher: Stephen York
Commissioning Editor: Deborah Parker
Map Editor: Bernard Horton

WHSmith
Siobhan Mulcahy
Kate Forster

Series Editor: Christopher Catling

Written and researched by: Eric and Ruth Bailey

Cover photograph: Caroline Jones

DISCOVER
DUBLIN

ERIC and RUTH BAILEY

Getting
to know
Dublin

Getting to know Dublin
Discovering Dublin

People from other parts of Ireland tend to dismiss Dublin as just another European city. Nothing could be further from the mark. True, it is metropolitan – cosmopolitan, even. True, it has the traffic snarl-ups you'll find in capital cities throughout the world (more than some, in fact). And it has those universal fast-food outlets, shopping malls and industrial parks.

Even so, it also has wide boulevards lined with trees and statues, elegant squares surrounded by fine, Georgian houses, and a river running through its heart. Paris? Vienna? A touch of London? They're all here, of course – but at heart Dublin remains essentially Irish.

Swift retribution?

Dublin is cheerful, individualistic, contrary, even perverse – the kind of place Jonathan Swift, author of *Gulliver's Travels*, might have invented. Maybe he did, for he lived, worked and wrote here as Dean of St Patrick's Cathedral in the first half of the 18th century.

Dublin is full of anomalies. Despite the shopping malls and burger palaces, it remains basically a city of small shops and street markets. Even the big shops – **Eason's** bookshop on O'Connell Street, for example, or the **Brown Thomas** department store on Grafton Street – have a small shop feel and offer small shop service.

Irish cuisine has undergone a renaissance in recent years and there are many restaurants offering top-class food, yet one of the city's favourite eating places is still **Beshoff's**, the fish and chip shop within a stone's throw of O'Connell Bridge.

Dublin's young people are as iconoclastic as any and they love the noisy discos and chic bistros of **Temple Bar**, but even the sophisticated undergraduates of **Trinity College** can be found gossiping loudly as they drink tea and eat sticky buns alongside older patrons among the potted palms in **Bewley's Café** on Grafton Street.

> **Johnson:** It [Ireland] is the last place where I should wish to travel.
> **Boswell:** Should you not like to see Dublin, sir.
> **Johnson:** No, sir. Dublin is only a worse capital.
>
> **James Boswell, *The Life of Johnson*, 1791**

The city has both the elegance of a princess and the shabbiness of a tramp. Behind some of those famous Georgian terraces lie noisy, noisome streets where dogs and horses – yes, horses! – roam free, and where you'd have to be mad to park a car. This is where the Dublin of James Joyce meets the Dublin of Roddy Doyle.

O'Connell Street, the widest in Europe at 150ft, with a strip of shady trees separating kerb from kerb, is the major link between the city's north and south. Like all good boulevards, it sweeps in genteel grandeur to meet a river.

No river dance

The Liffey is lined on both banks by quays that have witnessed the commerce of centuries. They still bustle with the movement of traffic and people, but the river is dead. Its only movement is the ebb and flow of the tides. There are no craft on it of any sort – no merchant vessels or dredgers; no trip boats, river buses or water taxis. Sadly, the Liffey now serves only as a focal point for tourists' cameras.

This then is the capital of Ireland. European, certainly. Irish, definitely. Perhaps Dublin is best symbolised by that famous cocktail, Black Velvet – a mixture of champagne and stout …

A day in the life of Dublin

There have been problems in the past – bitter strife, violence, economic depression – but Dublin today is a cheerful, buoyant place. It's a boom town full of Irish rovers, many of whom have returned home to enjoy the good life they once sought abroad.

Like the rest of Ireland, Dublin has seen its population growing again after decades of decline. Before the Great Famine of the 1840s the country's population was more than 6.5 million, but deaths from starvation and successive waves of emigration took such a toll that by 1961 there were only 2.8 million in Ireland.

Home again

Since the 1960s, increasing prosperity – the result of shrewd industrial development policies and judicious use of the perks of EU membership – has been attracting Irish men and women back home. By 1996 the population had climbed to around 3.6 million.

Today, Dublin is home to about a million happy-go-lucky souls who are clearly enjoying every moment of their country's success. They're a comparatively young lot: 44 per cent of Ireland's population is under the age of 25. Dublin, with **three universities** and a thriving range of **high-tech industries**, has an even higher proportion of young people.

It certainly shows. **Grafton Street** buzzes with the excitement of people eager to spend. **Temple Bar**, with its funky murals and Left Bank ambience, is electric from the determination of people to have fun. And in a typically Irish way, young Dubliners manage to be both dynamic and laid-back at the same time.

They're a loquacious bunch with a highly developed sense of fun, and a ready line of ironic repartee; jokes are often dismissive of pomposity and pretentiousness. They work hard at their city jobs, but lunchtime is sacrosanct and the pubs become noisily filled. The conversations, refreshingly, are about the gigs they attended last weekend, what they'll be doing tonight and the party they'll be going to on Saturday, rather than company closures and redundancy pay-offs.

The 'craic'

The pubs fill up again in the evening, the best time to see Dubliners at play. This is when they get together to enjoy 'the craic', that indefinable Irish phenomenon that means rather more than simply having a good time. Completely uninhibited, they'll join in a song – or get up and sing one themselves – at the drop of a hat, and they're always ready for a good-natured discussion on any subject you care to raise.

Dublin these days is a liberal city and subjects like sex, divorce and abortion are no longer off the agenda. Indeed, they are the stuff of nightly TV and radio talk shows. The Roman Catholic church has lost its intellectual grip on the people, and now there are no taboos.

St Patrick's Day

St Patrick's Day (17 March) is a public holiday in Ireland. In Dublin the celebrations last for days. The 1999 St Patrick's Festival started on Saturday, 13 March and didn't stop until the night of the following Wednesday. It marked the start of the city's Millennium Celebrations, with parades, pageantry, street theatre, music, dancing and fireworks.

Yesterday and tomorrow

Dublin celebrated its 1000th year in 1988, but its history goes back much further. Archaeological evidence suggests there were people living in the area as far back as 8000 BC, and Ptolemy's map of AD 140 shows a settlement named Eblana on the banks of the River Liffey.

People were drawn to the area by the abundance of fresh water created by the confluence of the rivers Liffey, Poddle, Dodder and Tolka, and it was the building of a ford of boughs and hurdles that gave the settlement its Irish name **Baile Átha Cliath** – the ford of hurdles – which appears on car licence plates in the city today. **'Dublin'** stems from the Gaelic words for 'a black pool' and the name dates from the 9th century when invading Vikings settled around such a pool near the present site of Dublin Castle.

The city's earliest inhabitants were pagan Celts, who readily accepted Christianity when **St Patrick** appeared in 432. According to legend, the saint himself baptised converts in a well close to where St Patrick's Cathedral now stands.

Viking raids

Scholarship flourished under Christianity and many of Ireland's monastic settlements were famed throughout Europe as centres of learning. The Vikings did their best to wreck it all, staging snap raids, destroying monasteries and villages and selling men, women and children into slavery. In Dublin the Irish and the Vikings gradually integrated, but strife continued. The budding city suffered constant attack from Irish armies, but in 1014 the Irish king **Brian Boru** put paid to the Scandinavians once and for all in the **Good Friday Battle of Clontarf**

Dublin enjoyed a century and a half of relative peace and quiet, a period which saw the foundation of **Christchurch Cathedral**. Then, in 1170, the city was taken by a Norman force from England, led by Robert de Clare, Earl of Pembroke, also known as **Strongbow**. It was the beginning of English control that was to last for more than 700 years.

Home rule for Ireland

Ireland saw constant unrest and rebellion under the English, but Dublin remained relatively stable, becoming established as the centre of political, economic and social life in the country.

By the 18th century the city had become a place of true cosmopolitan beauty, with wide streets and exquisite squares of elegant Georgian houses. But abolition of the Irish parliament and the **1800 Act of Union** with England caused Dublin to lose much of its importance and enter another period of decline.

The 19th century saw the rise of the middle classes and a growing pressure in Ireland for **Home Rule**. Dublin, enjoying the status of a provincial capital, was lukewarm, but public opinion was inflamed when leaders of the 1916 Easter Rising were executed by British firing squads in **Kilmainham Gaol**.

" *This was never my town,*
I was not born nor bred
Nor schooled here and she will not
Have me alive or dead.
But yet she holds my mind
With her seedy elegance. "
Louis MacNeice, Dublin, 1939

Ireland's **War of Independence** in 1921 and the bitter civil war that followed took a heavy toll on Dublin, which all but stagnated until the 1960s. Today, the city is vibrant, with a young well-educated population plugged in to the technology and promise of the 21st century.

People and places

Dubliners are proud that with a population of little more than a million their city has had a tremendous influence on world literature, drama and popular music. What other national capital has a museum devoted solely to its writers? Where else have so many internationally acclaimed rock and pop stars been produced that a special tourist trail has had to be created – and the way things are going is likely to be extended?

The writers

Generally regarded as the father of modern Irish literature, Jonathan Swift was born in Dublin in 1667. His birthplace in Hoey's Court, near Dublin Castle, no longer exists, but a bust of him can be found in St Patrick's Cathedral, where he served as Dean from 1713 until his death in 1745. Swift's wittily savage pen set the pace for modern satire.

The 19th-century poet James Clarence Mangan (1803–49), whose prolific output included *Dark Rosaleen* and *The Nameless One*, set a different kind of pace for Dublin's writers through an unquenchable need for strong drink. One of his favourite pubs was the Bleeding Horse, Camden Street, where they're still pulling pints to this day.

Master of the macabre Bram Stoker (1847–1912), creator of Count Dracula, was born at Clontarf, a northeast suburb. He worked in Dublin Castle as a civil servant before turning to writing. Although he spent much of his later years in London – to say nothing of Reading Gaol – Oscar Wilde (1854–1900) was born at 21 Westland Row and educated at Trinity College before gaining a scholarship to Magdalen College, Oxford.

The playwright George Bernard Shaw (1856–1950) was born at 33 Synge Street, now restored as a typical Victorian middle-class home and opened as the Shaw Birthplace Museum.

That colossus of Irish poetry, **William Butler Yeats**, was born in 1865 at 5 Sandymount Avenue, in the southeastern suburbs. He and Lady Gregory founded the Irish Literary Theatre at the old Abbey Theatre in 1904. One of their associates in the project was another Dubliner, the playwright **J M Synge** (1871–1909), author of *The Playboy of the Western World*. Yet another playwright associated with the Abbey was **Sean O'Casey**, author of *Juno and the Paycock*, who died in England in 1964. He was born at 85 Upper Dorset Street in 1880.

James Joyce, born at 41 Brighton Square, Rathgar, in 1882, was educated at University College, Dublin. He never set foot in Ireland after 1912. His first book of prose, *Dubliners*, was published in 1914 – but they say his masterpiece, *Ulysses* (1922), set on 16 June 1904, presents such a precise picture of Dublin that if the city were flattened it could be rebuilt brick by brick from his descriptions.

Other Dubliners who have made their mark on the 20th-century literary scene include Elizabeth Bowen, Samuel Beckett, Patrick Kavanagh, Brian O'Nolan (aka Flann O'Brien), and, of course, Brendan Behan, the roarin' writer who took up James Mangan's challenges of drink and ink.

Among those still bearing the literary torch are Roddy Doyle, John Banville, Derek Mahon, Eavan Boland and Seamus Heaney. Like Heaney, not all its writers have been native Dubliners, but they have embraced the city as warmly as it has embraced their success.

> *Eight o'clock. The streets were wet, puddles of water on the granite blocks. Western clouds swarming soundlessly catching up the turf smell from the steaming chimney pots on this chill Saturday night. Bird feet moving his soul through this Danish city.*
>
> **P Donleavy,**
> **The Ginger Man**

The musicians

It began in the 1960s with **The Chieftains** and **The Dubliners**, and their folk music challenge was picked up and carried along a rocking, rolling Celtic road by **Phil Lynott** and **Thin Lizzy**.

Others soon followed the trail, then set off on their own at a cracking pace: Bob Geldof and the **Boomtown Rats**, **U2**, **Moving Hearts** and **The Pogues**. In 1982 **Clannad** scored a hit with their *Theme from Harry's Game*, a strange, mystical lament with Gaelic lyrics. Milestones along the way include Sinéad O'Connor, Chris de Burgh, Enya, Hothouse Flowers, Something Happens!, The Cranberries, and, of course, *Riverdance*.

Getting around

Dublin is a compact city and most of its attractions are located in the centre, an area which can be strolled across comfortably within half an hour. For most people the easiest – and cheapest – way to get around is on foot. There are times, especially during the morning and afternoon rush hours, when it might also be the quickest.

Buses

Dublin Bus (Bus Átha Cliath) serves the city and suburbs with more than 100 routes. Services begin at 0630 and last buses leave at around 2330 (Sun from 1000). Passengers are expected to tender the exact fare to the driver. Pre-paid tickets are an easier, cheaper option.

is available, some also allowing unlimited travel on the suburban rail and rapid transit systems (*see opposite*). The Dublin Rambler card is good value for short-stay visitors. It offers three days of unlimited travel on all Dublin Bus services, including the Airlink service between the city centre and Dublin International airport, and can be bought at the Dublin Tourism centre, Suffolk Street, and more than 240 newsagents.

These, along with timetables and route maps, are available from **Dublin Bus**, *59 O'Connell Street; tel: 873 4222.*

A wide range of daily, weekly and monthly pre-paid tickets and passes

Nitelink, which is not covered by the Dublin Rambler, operates between midnight and 0300 along 15 routes to the suburbs on Thursdays, Fridays and Saturdays. The fare is considerably higher than during the day, so a family or other group might find it cheaper to travel by taxi.

Rail and DART

Suburban rail and DART (Dublin Area Rapid Transit) services are run by Iarnród Éireann and offer fast, clean and comfortable connections to some suburban districts and beyond. DART trains, which are very crowded during rush hours, run from about 0530 to midnight Mon–Sat and 0730–2330 Sun.

The DART system covers 25 stations between Howth in the north and Bray in the south, including Dún Laoghaire, the ferry port. It connects with mainline services at Dublin's Connolly Station and at Bray with trains to and from Rosslare and Wexford.

As with the buses, a variety of multi-trip ticket options is available. Suburban transport services, including buses, are divided into four 'hops' radiating from the city centre, with special-offer tickets priced accordingly. The Short Hop zone radiates north to Balbriggan, west to Maynooth and south to Kilcoole. The furthest zone, the Giant Hop, goes north to Dundalk, west to Mullingar and south to Gorey.

Special-offer tickets are available from all DART and suburban rail stations and from the **Rail Travel Centre** *35 Lower Abbey Street; tel: 836 6222.*

Taxis

According to legend, Dublin taxis may be hailed, but the fact is you'd stand a better chance searching for one among the official taxi ranks – and by the time you've found one of those you might have been better walking home. There are 24-hour ranks at Connolly and Heuston Stations, Westland Row Station, Aston Quay, Eden Quay and St Stephen's Green.

Taxi fares are relatively expensive, and much more so at night, on Sundays and public holidays. There are extra charges for additional passengers and for luggage stowed in the boot of the cab.

Rather than scour the streets, you could telephone one of the city's many taxi companies. Some will impose a pick-up charge. You could try the following: *285 5444* (**ABC**), *668 3333* (**Access and Metro Cabs**), *872 2688* (**City Cabs**), *661 2233* (**Pony Cabs**). Tip 10–15 per cent of the fare.

Bicycles

Apart from the risk of theft, cycling is a good way to get around Dublin. There are no really steep hills, and in general it is faster than motoring in the city centre. You can rent bikes from **Dublin Bike Hire**: *tel: 878 8473*, and **C Harding for Bicycles**: *tel: 873 2455.*

Horse power

Sightseeing tours by horse-drawn cab start at Fusiliers' Arch, opposite Grafton Street at the northwest corner of St Stephen's Green, and are a pleasant way to see the city's streets when the weather is fair.

Car hire

Major car hire companies have desks at Dublin International Airport and at Dublin Port and Dún Laoghaire ferry ports. **Dan Dooley Car Hire**, an old-established Irish company, has its town centre office in Westland Row, near Pearse Station: *tel: 677 2723.*

Driving

The rules of the road in Ireland are much the same as those in the United Kingdom. Drive on the left, overtake on the right. At roundabouts give way to traffic coming from the right. Speed limits are 30mph (50kmh) in built-up areas, 60mph (95kmh) outside built-up areas, and 70mph (110kmh) on motorways. Distances can be a problem. The republic's newest signs, in green and white, show distances in kilometres; older black and white signs give miles.

There are good, fast roads in Dublin's outer reaches. The M50 motorway will eventually encircle the city, providing links with all the major routes inland. At present it extends from just northeast of Dublin airport to Tallaght in the southwest suburbs – about three-quarters of its proposed distance. North of the city, the M50 links with the M1 and N1 north to Belfast and the N2 to Derry; to the west and southwest it connects with the N4 to Galway and the N7, the major highway to Limerick and routes to Waterford and Cork.

In the city itself, the best advice is unless you really need to drive – don't. Road surfaces and traffic controls are good, but signage is weak in places and the sheer volume of traffic, even in spacious O'Connell Street, can make driving a misery.

At peak times it can take up to half an hour to drive from the Parnell Monument to O'Connell Bridge, an easy 10-minute stroll.

Car parking in the city centre is difficult and expensive.

Guided tours

You can gain a good introduction to the city by joining the Hop on-Hop off tour run by Dublin Bus. The complete tour lasts about 75 minutes, but you can take all day over it, if you wish, hopping on and off at any of 12 stops, each conveniently located near one of the city's most popular attractions. The open-top buses depart hourly from outside *59 O'Connell Street; tel: 873 4222*, and your ticket entitles you to a discount at some of the attractions en route.

For a guided cycling tour contact **Dublin Bike Tours**: *tel: 679 0899*.

A genial insight into Dublin's literature, history and architecture is provided on the **Jameson Dublin Literary Pub Crawl**: *tel: 454 0228*. The tours take place-round and are led by actors who play some of the city's most colourful characters as groups progress from pub to pub, starting at The Duke on Duke Street.

Maps and information

Before you go

Irish Tourist Board: *Ireland House, 150–151 New Bond Street, London W1Y 0AQ.*
Tel: 0171 493 3201.
Fax: 0171 493 9065.

When you're there

Dublin Tourism Centre: *Suffolk Street, Dublin 2. Tel: 605 7799. E-mail: reservations@dublintourism.ie*

The following information and reservations centres are for personal callers only: Dublin Airport; Baggott Street Bridge; Dún Laoghaire Ferry Terminal; Exclusively Irish, O'Connell Street; The Square, Town Centre, Tallaght.

Don't miss

1 Ha'penny Bridge

Cross the River Liffey on Dublin's most enduring and endearing image, the elegantly bowed Wellington Bridge (to give it its official name when it opened in 1816), take in the views on either side and smile, as everyone does.
Page 33

2 Kilmainham Gaol

There's not much to smile about in here, where the leaders of the 1916 Easter Rising were executed, but the grim place does present a poignant picture of Ireland's often sad and violent past. **Pages 116-117**

3 Dublin Writers Museum

Rare books and manuscripts are on show in this restored Georgian mansion, a restrained celebration of the city's many literary giants. **Pages 28-29**

4 Christ Church Cathedral

The cathedral was founded in 1172 on the site of a wooden church built in 1038 by Sitric Silkenbeard, king of the Dublin Norsemen. The massive Norman edifice houses the tomb of Strongbow, the Earl of Pembroke. **Pages 92-93**

5 St Patrick's Cathedral

Close your eyes and imagine St. Patrick himself baptising pagan converts in a nearby well. A church has stood on this site since 450, and Jonathan Swift, Dean of the cathedral for more than 30 years, is buried in the nave. **Pages 94-95**

6 Trinity College

This is how a university should look. While you're there, check out the entertaining multimedia presentation, *Dublin Experience*. And don't forget the *Book of Kells*.
Pages 44-45, 50-51

7 Grafton Street

Let your credit card run free in Dublin's shopping heart. You can also enjoy entertaining busking, great people-watching and superb pubs. **Pages 52–65**

8 Marsh's Library

Ireland's first public library had been opened for 13 years when Jonathan Swift was appointed Dean of neighbouring St Patrick's Cathedral in 1713. With 25,000 rare books and manuscripts, you can understand why they locked the readers in cages. **Page 99**

9 James Joyce Tower

Take a trip to the nearby seaside suburb of Sandycove to see the Martello tower which became the setting for the opening chapter of *Ulysses* after Joyce stayed there with Oliver St John Gogarty in 1904. **Page 130**

10 Guinness Hop Store

Find out how 'the black stuff' is made and try a sip or three while you're about it .
Page 119

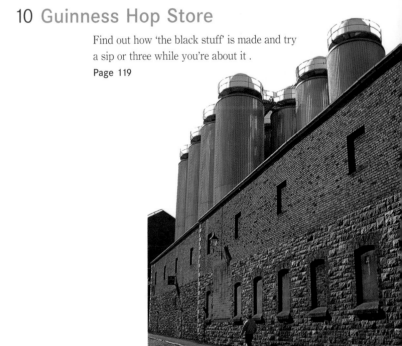

☞ *The Guinness Brewery*

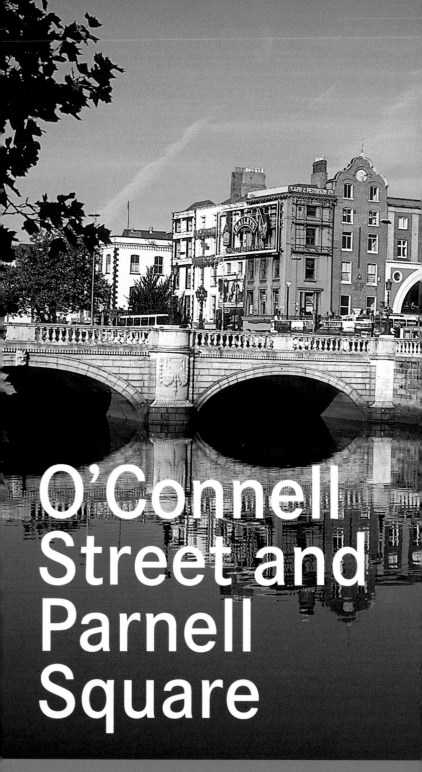

O'Connell Street and Parnell Square

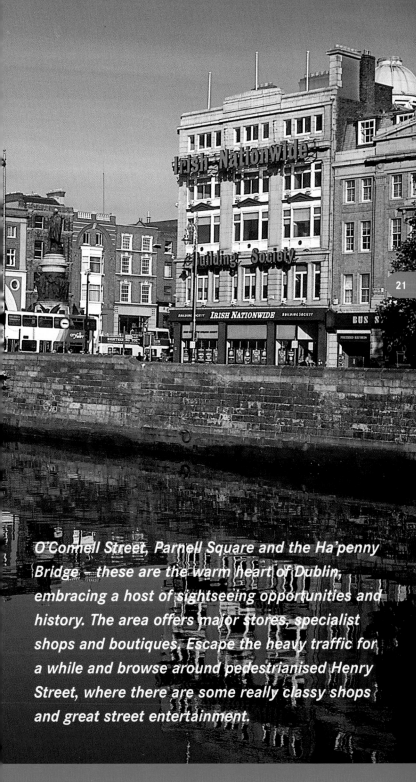

O'Connell Street, Parnell Square and the Ha'penny Bridge – these are the warm heart of Dublin, embracing a host of sightseeing opportunities and history. The area offers major stores, specialist shops and boutiques. Escape the heavy traffic for a while and browse around pedestrianised Henry Street, where there are some really classy shops and great street entertainment.

O'CONNELL STREET AND PARNELL SQUARE

Getting there: virtually all Dublins public transport systems meet just east of O'Connell Street: the bus station is three blocks east on Store Street, and the Tara Street Station, on the south bank of the Liffey, brings DART passengers into the city centre.

O'CONNELL STREET AND PARNELL SQUARE

① *Ha'penny Bridge*

The most photographed bridge in Dublin must surely be the picturesque Ha'penny Bridge, whose graceful arch spans the river between Temple Bar and Liffey Street. It is the river's only pedestrian bridge. **Page 33**

② *Abbey Theatre*

Irish pride is almost tangible here. The theatre stages works by Ireland's literary greats and encourages the up-and-coming generation of the nation's writers. **Page 33**

③ *Dublin Writers Museum*

Meet James, Samuel, Oscar, Sean and all the top literary figures of Ireland, mostly from the past, of course, but including recent Nobel prize-winner Seamus Heaney. A personal stereo commentary introduces each writer as you study their photographs, portraits, original letters and a few personal possessions. **Pages 28–29**

④ *Barrows and banter*

One of the liveliest corners of a lively city is at the Moore Street Market. The cacophany of street cries as stallholders offer their produce makes great entertainment. Shopping doesn't normally offer much humour and good-natured banter, but at Moore Street you get a laugh along with your lettuces. **Page 25**

⑤ *Peace and quiet*

The Garden of Remembrance provides a place to rest and reflect. On the site where the Irish Volunteers movement was formed, it commemorates all those who died in the cause of Irish freedom. In the clear waters of a pool, peace is depicted by a mosaic of thrown-away swords and weapons. **Page 26**

⑥ *Ulysses et al*

Aficionados attend lectures at the James Joyce Centre to get a deeper insight into his work. A series of biographies of nearly 50 real Dubliners on whom Joyce based his best-known work, *Ulysses*, can be studied. **Page 32**

⑦ *Fountain with female*

A slightly whimsical portrayal of James Joyce's character, Anna Livia, was fashioned to represent the River Liffey. The statue was unveiled in 1988 to mark Dublin's millennium. Give the lady a smile as you walk by. **Page 24**

⑧ *A place to shop*

Much of O'Connell Street was rebuilt in the 1920s and 1930s, following damage to properties during the 1916 Easter Rising. Some of the older buildings remain, giving the street a mix of architecture. One survivor is Clery's department store, dating from 1822; good for a browse around – the Irish knitwear is tempting. **Page 37**

O'Connell Street

The O'Connell Bridge over the River Liffey forms a dividing line between the north and the south of Dublin. O'Connell Street, on the north side, dates from the 1700s. It was one of the early boulevard streets

developed in a number of Europe's notable cities. The 150ft-wide thoroughfare is divided by a pedestrian island. The island has several statues and memorials. The latest is the Anna Livia Millennium Fountain, unveiled in 1988 to mark Dublin's millennium. The locals, with their irreverent humour, have dubbed it 'the Floozie in the Jacuzzi'. Near by, at North Earl Street, is Marjorie Fitzgibbon's statue of Anna's creator, James Joyce.

O'Connell Bridge

Named the Carlisle Bridge when it was built in the 1790s, the O'Connell Bridge was renamed in 1882 after **Daniel O'Connell**, anti-Union politician and lawyer who helped bring about Catholic emancipation. A memorial statue to O'Connell was erected near the bridge more than 30 years after his death.

More monuments

At the junction of Parnell Square with O'Connell Street is a tall monument to **Charles Stewart Parnell,** the politician who negotiated with Gladstone's government at Westminster and almost won Home Rule. But at a crucial moment he was spurned by everyone – Gladstone, his own party members and the Church – because he had fallen in love with a married woman and was cited in a divorce case. His career in ruins, Parnell was a broken man. His health deteriorated and he died soon afterwards in 1891 at the age of 45.

Shops and markets

While it could hardly be called tranquil, Henry Street, off O'Connell Street, is traffic-free, which makes shopping quicker and more pleasurable. It's a great place for fashion, jewellery, quality gifts and souvenirs. All you need is money. The lilting Irish music of buskers should put a spring in your step.

Moore Street, off O'Connell Street, presents an artist's palette of colour with its lively market, assailing your senses of smell and hearing as well as sight. The heady scent of mixed cut flowers, the street vendors' raucous cries and their persuasive patter make this an exciting spot for market addicts. Barrow-loads of fresh fruit and vegetables occupy the Moore Street Market, and there are also fish and meat outlets.

Dublin's boulevards

Dublin has a maze of narrow lanes and alleys, but its most striking feature is the number of streets of boulevard proportions. These were created by the Wide Streets Commissioners, a body founded by Act of Parliament in 1757. Parliament Street, leading from Grattan Bridge to Dublin Castle, was opened in 1762. Dame Street followed in 1769. Sackville Street (now Lower O'Connell Street) was completed in 1784, and other developments continued until 1800.

Parnell Square

Dating from the 1750s and originally named Rutland Square, Parnell Square provided a prestigious address for aristocrats, MPs, men of the ecclesiastical hierarchy and other notables. In a city of fine Georgian architecture, the Square stands out as a peaceful area of gracious buildings, and provides a contrast with the commercial activities and jostling crowds of O'Connell Street, just round the corner.

Garden of Remembrance

This small public park developed as a memorial to the men and women who died for Irish freedom. It was opened in 1966, marking the 50th anniversary of the Easter Rising. The ancient Irish legend of the *Children of Lir*, four children whose cruel stepmother turned them into swans for nine centuries, is depicted in an impressive **bronze sculpture** by Oisin Kelly. W B Yeats's poem about the Easter Rising of 1916 is also illustrated in a sculpture here.

General Post Office

Tel: 705 7000. Mon–Sat 0800–2000, Sun 1000–1830.

Modern Irish history is firmly stamped on O'Connell Street. The General Post Office was significantly involved in the **Easter Rising** of 1916. You can go in to buy stamps for your postcards or make a phone call from the row of coin and card phones and see the **bullet holes** in the portico columns.

The Irish Volunteer Force was set up in Dublin in 1913 to defend the claim to Home Rule and to oppose the notion of Home Rule of the armed Ulster Volunteer Force. The vast majority of the Irish Volunteers, however, (about 200,000), were persuaded to fight in World War I against the Germans. This left only about 10,000 to act as a national defence force. It was decided to organise a rising while Britain was busy fighting against Germany. The **Proclamation of a Republic** was read outside the GPO on Easter Monday 1916.

Nelson toppled

In the early 1800s a 134ft pillar topped by a statue of Horatio Nelson was erected near the GPO at the intersection of North Earl Street and Henry Street. It commemorated his victory at the Battle of Trafalgar, but in March 1966, just before the 50th anniversary of the Easter Rising of 1916, it was blown up. Dublin's best-known landmark was destroyed. Nelson's head of Portland stone now rests in the Civic Museum.

Many O'Connell Street buildings were severely damaged in the fierce battle that followed. In less than a week, under heavy attack by British troops and with many civilian casualties, the rebels had to surrender. Fourteen of the leaders of the Rising were executed within three weeks of that Easter Monday bloodbath.

Around Parnell Square

Rotunda Hospital

In the mid 18th century many Dublin women died in childbirth, and the number of stillbirths was high. Bartholomew Mosse, a doctor specialising in midwifery, bought a site and set up a committee of friends to form an entertainment centre and pleasure gardens with which to fund a maternity hospital. Formerly known as the Lying-in Hospital, and claimed to be the first of its kind in Europe, the Rotunda Hospital rarely lost a life. It took its name from the opulent **Rotunda Room** which had been a concert venue and has been a cinema since 1913.

The hospital building can be viewed from the outside (there is no public admission). It was designed by Mosse's friend, Richard Cassells, who died before adding the magnificent **chapel**, which has some internationally esteemed features.

Gate Theatre

The famous little Gate Theatre was known as the Assembly Rooms when it was completed in 1786 as the Supper Room in the Rotunda Hospital. It was not until 1930 that it was converted to a theatre and quickly gained a high reputation for staging important European productions. Two international stars who cut their thespian teeth at the Gate were **James Mason** and **Orson Welles**.

Dublin Writers Museum

18 Parnell Square North. Tel: 872 2077. Mon–Sat 1000–1700, Sun and public holidays 1100–1700, June–Aug until 1800. Admission: ££.

At the Square's northern end, the Dublin Writers Museum provides two pleasures. Not only can you study original letters, profiles, portraits, memorabilia and photographs of three centuries of the major figures on the city's literary stage, but you can also see the lavishly ornamented colonnade and gilded frieze in the **Writers Gallery** upstairs. This was the work of Manchester architect Alfred Darbyshire who was called in to make alterations to the house, built around 1780, when it was bought by George Jameson, a member of the Irish whiskey family, in 1891. The work took four years.

The Writers Museum was opened by Dublin Tourism in 1991 as its contribution to Dublin's year as European City of Culture. Four of the writers featured – **Yeats**, **Shaw**, **Beckett** and **Heaney** – have been awarded the Nobel Prize for Literature. Audio equipment provided at the desk gives a gentle commentary on what you are seeing, without going into too much detail. It enables you to be selective and to spend as much or as little time with each writer as you want.

After spending time with James Joyce, Samuel Beckett, J M Synge, Jonathan Swift, George Bernard Shaw, Richard Brinsley Sheridan, John Kavanagh, Oscar Wilde and others, you may like to refresh the inner self at the museum's **Coffee Shop**.

National Wax Museum

Granby Row, Parnell Square. Tel: 872 6340. Mon–Sat 1000–1730, Sun 1200–1730. Admission: ££.

Meet some of the people who have shaped Ireland's history at the National Wax Museum. Celebrities from the worlds of politics, literature, drama, sport, music and other fields stand before you as you listen to their biographies. There's a **chamber of horrors** and a captivating section for **children**.

❝ *We pleased ourselves with the spectacle of Dublin's commerce – the barges signalled from far away by their curls of woolly smoke, the brown fishing fleet beyond Ringsend, the big, white sailing vessel which was being discharged on the opposite quay.* **❞**

James Joyce, *Dubliners*

Hugh Lane Municipal Gallery of Modern Art

This fine museum is named after its benefactor who, in 1905, decided to donate his collection of Impressionist works to Dublin Corporation, with the proviso that they should be exhibited in a suitable building. The Corporation dragged its heels in finding an appropriate place, so Sir Hugh, losing patience, thought he would let London have the gift instead.

Later he had second thoughts and reverted to his original plan. He added a codicil to his will to this effect, but before it was witnessed, Sir Hugh met an untimely death – he was a passenger on the *Lusitania* when it was torpedoed in World War I.

It took lawyers half a century to sort it out, though nobody was entirely happy with the outcome: Dublin and London should take turns to show items from the collection.

This means that you can never be sure entirely what will be on display at the time of your visit, but whatever is on display will be worth seeing. Hugh Lane collected the work of his contemporaries, including many **Impressionists**. Part of the reason for the legal wrangling was that Impressionist art was not highly regarded at the time. Not everybody was convinced of its merits as art. Today, of course, the Impressionists are fetching record prices at auction. This gallery nearly always has one or two well-known works on display, as well as a noted collection of 20th-century modern and contemporary art. It also has temporary exhibitions of works by modern artists from Europe and further afield. Don't miss the stained glass section or the sculpture hall.

The building that houses the gallery is also of interest. **Charlemont House** was built for James Caulfield, Earl of Charlemont, in 1761–3. The architect was Sir William Chambers, who also designed Lord Charlemont's Italianate-style house, Marino Casino. Charlemont House was considered one of the finest in Dublin at a time when many splendid houses were being built for the wealthy and influential. It became a gallery of modern art in 1932. A bookshop and café are on the premises.

Free Sunday **concerts** of contemporary music often take place in a large hall at the gallery, mainly between September and June. For dates and details of these tel: 677 1717. For information on visiting art exhibitions tel: 874 1903.

Charlemont House, Parnell Square.
Tel: 874 1903. Tue–Fri 0930–1800,
Sat 0930–1700, Sun 1100–1700.
Closed Mon. Free.

66 *Nearly all young Irishmen keep one eye on the possibility of emigrating. They look upon their life in Ireland as a transitory fact.* 99

D P Moran,
The Philosophy
of Irish Ireland, 1898

Around O'Connell Street

James Joyce Centre

35 North Great George's Street. Tel: 878 8547. Mon–Sat 0930–1700, Sun 1230–1700. Admission: £.

The James Joyce Centre is one of the carefully restored Georgian houses in the street. In the reference library and exhibition rooms you can get to know much about Joyce and his work. He obviously believed that to write about a place you need to distance yourself from it. Joyce lived abroad, yet always wrote about Dublin. His magnum opus, *Ulysses*, tells of one Dublin day, as experienced by many local characters. The book was considered pornographic and remained on the banned list in Ireland until 1960. Joyce died in 1941.

You may even meet relatives of the writer, who are on the centre's staff. Tours of **Joyce's Dublin** begin here.

Capel Street

Meetinghouse Lane. Tel: 872 1490. Wed and Sun 1000–1700, mid June–mid Sept.

Capel Street is one of the city centre's busy shopping and commercial streets. St Mary's Abbey, dating from the 12th century, is just off here in Meetinghouse Lane. The remains of the entrance to the old Chapter House of the Cistercian Abbey, dissolved around 1530, can be seen. An exhibition on its history is open Wednesday and Sunday from mid June to mid September.

Abbey Theatre

26 Lower Abbey Street. Tel: 878 7222 (box office).

Leading off the southern end of O'Connell Street is Lower Abbey Street, home of the world famous, century-old Abbey Theatre, which incorporates the **Peacock Theatre**. It was founded in 1904 by W B Yeats, Lady Augusta Gregory and Edward Martyn, and was originally known as the Irish National Theatre. The present theatre was purpose-built, reopening in 1966, a full 15 years after a fire which forced the evacuation of the theatre to other venues.

The Abbey promotes the works of new Irish writers as well as Irish classics, and also commissions new young writers and holds workshops to encourage and help budding playwrights.

> **"** *At an Abbey Theatre performance, when I was in Dublin earlier this year, I discovered I cannot sit through 'Cathleen na Houlihan' without crying ... I think it is chiefly for the single reason that the history of Ireland is unbearably sad ...* **"**
>
> **Brigid Brophy, 1966**

Ha'penny Bridge

Links Batchelors Row to Wellington Quay.

Officially it's the Wellington Bridge, named after the Duke of Wellington who died in 1852, but everybody knows it as the Ha'penny Bridge, so called because in days gone by that was the toll charged for crossing it (the toll ceased in 1919). A beautiful structure with elegant lamps, the bridge opened in 1816, and was cast at Coalville, in Shropshire. As the only footbridge over the River Liffey it is a much-loved Dublin landmark.

Custom House

Splendidly impressive, reflected in the waters of the River Liffey, the magnificent neo-classical Custom House has stood for more than two centuries. It was designed by the architect James Gandon (see pages 38–39) and was opened in 1791, replacing a building at Wellington Quay where cargoes could be loaded and unloaded close to the city's commercial centre. Many people involved in commerce opposed the new site nearer the mouth of the river and hired mobs to attack the builders.

O'CONNELL STREET AND PARNELL SQUARE

> *The Dublin of old statues, this arrogant city, stirs proudly and secretly in my blood.* **99**
>
> **Donagh McDonagh, in the poem *Dublin Made Me***

Gandon had to lay elaborate foundations as the building was constructed on a sandy site. In 1838 a fire caused serious though not devastating damage, but in 1921, in the War of Independence, Nationalists started a fire which was far more destructive. Repair work took five years and cost £300,000.

Nearly 50 years later, in the 1970s, cracks in the stonework indicated that the effects of the fire were still taking its toll. A huge restoration programme in the 1980s was completed in time for the Custom House's bicentenary in 1991.

Today, a visitor centre in the dome and clock tower area is open daily to the public. The building's history is outlined and a museum features a display on Gandon and his life and work in Ireland.

Custom House Quay. Tel: 878 7660. Mid Mar–Nov Mon–Fri 1000–1700, Sat–Sun 1400–1700; Nov–mid Mar Wed–Fri 1000–1700, Sun 1400–1700. Admission: £.

Eating and drinking

Global Internet Café

8 Lower O'Connell Street, Dublin 3. Tel: 878 0233. £. Go surfing and enjoy a meal here, too. The food and coffee are popular, even with non-nerds, and there are e-mail and internet facilities.

Beshoff's Restaurant

Lower O'Connell Street. Tel: 462 4181. £. This long-established restaurant claims to serve the best fish and chips in Dublin. Interesting tiled décor, good service.

Bangkok Café

106 Parnell Street, Dublin 2. Tel: 878 6618. ££. Modestly-priced high-quality Thai food is served here. Open for dinner from 1730, it is very popular with Dubliners. You'll need to book.

Chapter One

18 Parnell Square, Dublin 1. Tel: 873 2266. ££. Located in the basement of the Dublin Writers Museum, it's big and intimate at the same time, thanks to the way it is divided up into little rooms accessed by archways. The food is divine.

Juice

South Great George Street, Dublin 2. Tel: 475 7856. ££. Serves good vegetarian meals at remarkably low prices. The wine may be produced organically. *Open 0900–2300 or later.*

Winding Stair

40 Ormond Quay, Dublin 1. Tel: 873 3292. £. Bookshops which serve coffee have become fashionable. At this one, near Ha'penny Bridge, you can lunch on soup and sandwiches and look out on the Liffey. No booze, but the coffee is good. *Open to 1800.*

The early bird

No self-respecting Irishman or woman thinks in terms of a mere sandwich for lunch. If it's not a knife and fork job it doesn't really count. Even so, the Irish are ready for another meal early in the evening. Pubs are great places for a sustaining stoke-up, but you'll have to be there early. A few serve hot food up to 2130, but even in a livewire city like Dublin more tend to start early, around 1700, and close their kitchens by 1930 or 2000.

If you want to eat late, you'll find plenty of Temple Bar and city centre cafés and restaurants serving food until midnight. It's wise to book if you can.

Shopping

O'Connell Street has a good mix of shops. The main department store is **Clery's***, which has a craft shop.* **Eason and Sons'** *spacious bookshop has a large section devoted to Irish history, politics, landscape, legends, literature and just about every aspect of Ireland. If you can't find what you want here, it probably doesn't exist. There's a good choice of maps and posters, too.*

Photographic equipment, jewellery, fashions for all age groups, shoes, backpacks and leather goods, are all available in O'Connell Street itself or its offshoots, such as Henry Street, and the Abbey Mall between Abbey Street and Lotts.

Art works can be bought at galleries either side of the Liffey in the vicinity of the Ha'penny Bridge, where there is a variety of antique and collectables shops and other specialist stores. **The Dublin Woollen Mills** shop is enticing, with traditional Irish knitwear and expensive sports jackets. Outside it is a modern sculpture of two women shoppers, affectionately called 'the hags with the bags' by Dubliners.

Even if you don't play an instrument, you'll find a fascinating range of Irish harps, pipes, flutes, fiddles, accordions and bodhrans – small goatskin drums – at **Walton's** in North Frederick Street which has been trading for more than 75 years. There are CDs and cassettes of Irish music.

McDowell's, in Upper O'Connell Street, sells gold and silver hand-crafted souvenir jewellery and Waterford crystal. A mailing service is offered.

Designs on Dublin

James Gandon, born in 1742, was a successful London architect in his 30s, poised to go to the Russian city of St Petersburg to work on a major project. Then he was invited to Dublin to build a new Custom House *(see pages 34–35). Ireland evidently appealed to him more than Russia because he declined the St Petersburg job and accepted the Dublin invitation. He was to spend the rest of his days in Ireland, becoming the architect of some of the city's most prestigious buildings.*

At Inns Quay, the **Four Courts** (*see page 110*) – Chancery, King's Bench, Exchequer and Common Pleas – are considered by some to be Gandon's finest work. The project took more than five years to complete and cost £200,000, an unimaginable fortune in those days.

O'CONNELL STREET AND PARNELL SQUARE

During his early days in Dublin Gandon and Robert Parke were asked to enlarge Parliament House on College Green, opposite the entrance to Trinity College. It has been used as the head office of the **Bank of Ireland** (*see page 46*) since 1808.

Gandon's final major public building, constructed in his mid-60s, was the **King's Inns**, begun in 1795 (*see page 110*). It was not a sublime experience for him. Frustrated by a series of obstacles and delays, he threw in the towel 13 years after the foundation stone was laid. His partner and pupil, Henry Aaron Baker, completed the work to Gandon's design in 1816.

Behind the Custom House is the Central Bus Station of Busaras, with office block, which was one of the first major modern buildings in Dublin. The grand structure was designed by Michael Scott and opened in 1953. In the 1930s Scott designed his own home, a white tower house which catches the eye at Sandycove Beach.

As well as public buildings, Gandon was responsible for a number of Dublin's gracious homes, notably the crescent of houses in **Beresford Place**.

He was over 80 when he died at his home, Canonbrook. His grave is at Drumcondra, about 3 miles north of the city centre.

Dublin's Academia

Viewed from College Green, where its main entrance is flanked by statues of Edmund Burke and Oliver Goldsmith, Trinity College seems a sombre, institutional place. But pass through the tight formality of its gate and you enter a world of spacious elegance – a transition that seems to symbolise the widening of intellectual horizons.

DUBLIN'S ACADEMIA

BEST OF
Dublin's
Academia

Getting there: Trinity College lies two blocks south of the Tara Street DART station, and can be reached by any bus that passes through Dublin city centre.

0   500m

0   500 yds

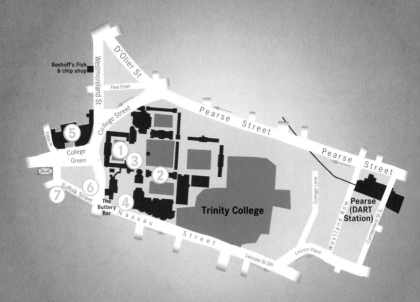

Beshoff's Fish
& chip shop

D'Olier St

Westmoreland St

Fleet Street

College Street

Pearse   Street

Pearse   Street

Pearse   Street

5

College
Green

1

3

2

College Lane

Westland Row

Pearse
(DART
Station)

Cumberland S S

6

7

Suffolk Street

The
Buttery
Bar

4

N a s s a u   Street

Trinity College

Leinster St Sth

Lincoln Place

① Parliament Square

Front Gate, Trinity's tunnel-like main entrance, emerges into cobbled Parliament Square. Dominated by a 98ft-high campanile and encompassing swathes of neat lawn, as well as imposing college buildings, the square is massive. **Pages 44–45**

② The Book of Kells

Ireland's most famous medieval book, the richly decorated illuminated manuscript from the 9th century, is housed inside Trinity's Old Library, with other priceless treasures from the past, including a harp dating from the 15th century. The Old Library is a very popular attraction, so get here early to avoid the crowds, especially during peak holiday times. **Pages 50–51**

③ Examination Hall

This is a magnificently distracting room in which to sit your finals, with superb ceilings to stare at while you try to think of the answer. **Page 45**

④ Dublin Experience

Romp through 1000 years of the city's history with this good-humoured and informative audio-visual presentation in the Thomas Davis Theatre on the Trinity campus. **Page 45**

⑤ Bank of Ireland

The Bank of Ireland building on College Green must be one of the grandest of its kind anywhere in the world. It was completed in 1739 as Europe's first purpose-built parliament building and became a bank after the Irish Parliament voted itself out of existence. **Page 46**

⑥ Molly Malone

Pay your respects to the buxom fishmonger, Molly Malone, pushing her wheelbarrow on the corner of Grafton and Suffolk streets. The bronze statue is known as 'the dish with the fish', though less reverent Dubliners call it 'the tart with the cart'. **Pages 46–47**

⑦ Dublin Tourism

Located in the former St Andrew's Church, in Suffolk Street, the Dublin Tourism Centre has become a tourist attraction in its own right, with many of its original 19th-century architectural features tastefully retained. **Page 47**

43

Trinity College

Queen Elizabeth I founded Trinity College in 1592 and women were admitted as students in 1903. The total student population now numbers around 8000. Among its most famous graduates are Jonathan Swift, Bram Stoker, Oscar Wilde and Samuel Beckett. Trinity's campus (*open at all times*) covers 42 acres of cobbled squares, gardens and sports grounds.

Front Gate

Stone likenesses of two of Dublin's literary giants of the 18th century flank Trinity's main entrance. On the left, as you face the gate, is a statue of **Edmund Burke** (1729–97), the political writer who became a British Member of Parliament.

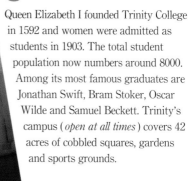

On the right is **Oliver Goldsmith** (1728–74), poet and playwright. Both men studied at Trinity. The statues are the work of John Foley and were completed in the 1860s. Foley must have used the same model for the lower half of each statue – the two figures have identical legs.

Parliament Square

None of the college's original Elizabethan buildings has survived, but their loss has been amply compensated by the magnificent Palladian structures surrounding Parliament Square, so called because much of its cost was met by the 18th-century Irish government. If the scene seems familiar, it's probably because this was where much of the 1983 film *Educating Rita* was shot.

Facing each other beyond the first pair of lawns are the **Examination Hall** and the **Chapel**, both designed by Sir William Chambers. Completed in 1791, the Examination Hall has ornate ceilings and a gilded oak chandelier that once hung in the old Irish House of Commons, and was designed to double up as a theatre. For many years, the impressive organ was said to have come from a Spanish ship, but it is now believed to have been built in Dublin in 1684 by Lancelot Pease, who also undertook work at King's College, Cambridge.

The Chapel was designed to match the Examination Hall and was completed in 1798. It features fine plasterwork and stained glass and is a popular site for up-market weddings.

Parliament Square is dominated by the massive campanile donated in 1853 by the Archbishop of Armagh and designed by Sir Charles Lanyon, architect of Queen's University, Belfast.

Library Square

College Green. Tel: 608 2308. Mon–Sat 0930–1700; Sun 1200–1630 (Oct–May), 0930–midnight (June–Sept).

The lawned area behind the campanile is known as Library Square, and the row of redbrick buildings at the far end are the **Rubrics**, the oldest surviving buildings in the college, dating from 1700.

To the right of the Rubrics is the Old Library, built in 1732, which contains the magnificent Long Room, the largest single chamber library in Europe, measuring 213ft by 42ft. On the ground floor, **The Colonnades** exhibition gallery displays the world-famous *Book of Kells*, the 9th-century illuminated manuscript of the Four Gospels (*see pages 50–51*). Other early Christian manuscripts are also on show, together with Ireland's oldest harp, dating from the 15th century and featured on the country's coinage.

Beyond Library Square are Trinity's newer developments, including New Square (1838–44) and the Berkeley Library Building (1967). The Thomas Davis Theatre houses the audio-visual presentation, the **Dublin Experience**, an entertaining outline of the city's history over the past 1000 years (*open daily mid May–Sept, 1000–1700; admission: ££*).

Around College Green

Bank of Ireland

2 College Green. Tel: 677 7801. Mon–Wed and Fri 1000–1600, Thur 1000–1700. Free.

Said to be one of Europe's greatest public buildings, this was originally the purpose-built Irish Parliament House. It was also Dublin's first Palladian-style building, designed by the young architect Edward Lovett Pearce, who died before it was completed. Later extensions were designed by **James Gandon** (*see page 38*). The building was sold to the Bank of Ireland after the Irish Parliament was dissolved in 1800. The former House of Commons is now the Banking Mall, while the House of Lords, resplendently intact with magnificent woodwork and ceilings, fine tapestries and a beautiful chandelier, offers guided tours – ask the security staff.

Molly Malone

She's haunted the corner of Grafton Street and Suffolk Street since 1988 – the brassy, buxom woman who has stamped an indelible nostalgia on the city's soul. Sweet Molly Malone, as frozen as her fish would be if she sold them today, is as

much a part of Irish mythology as Cuchulain, the super-hero of Celtic legend. Many Dubliners swear she was a real 17th- or 18th-century fishmonger who, like so many of her contemporaries, 'died of a fever' after a short lifetime of cripplingly hard work. Less romantic critics say she was a 'woman of the night' who got no more than she deserved. Either way, there's much food for thought as you ponder Molly and her laden barrow.

Suffolk Street

Most of Dublin's tourists find themselves 'attending church' in Suffolk Street. The former Protestant church of St Andrew is now the **Dublin Tourism Centre**. Built in 1866, St Andrew's was the latest in a series of churches which had stood on or near the site since the 11th century.

> *It is unforgettably a capital. Soldiers appear and reappear like monotonous red toys, under the shadow of the low cleric temple that is now the Bank of Ireland but that once was the Irish Parliament House.*
>
> **Essayist Robert Lynd, from *Home Life in Ireland*, 1908**

After it closed, the building's future was in doubt, and one fear was that it would be turned into a disco. Finally, in December 1994, St Andrew's reopened as the city's major tourism centre. Still very much a Church of Ireland building in character, it has been cleverly converted, with staffed information and accommodation reservation desks, a bookshop, souvenir and gift shops, a bureau de change and a car rental company.

Details of bus tours and services are available, ticket reservations can be made and there are brochures and leaflets on scores of attractions, excursions by bus and rail, and tourist information covering all Ireland as well as the Dublin area. Upstairs, the **Belfry Café** provides hot and cold meals and refreshments.

Just around the corner from the tourism centre are the offices of **Hot Press** (*13 Trinity Street*), the controversial magazine which has become the authoritative international voice of Irish rock music. Its writers have a reputation for spotting embryonic talent.

Eating and drinking

Around Trinity College you'll find all the ingredients that make up the quintessential student lifestyle – vegetarian restaurants, affordable pub grub, trendy coffee bars, and smoky pubs where intellectual academics rub shoulders with jaded journalists.

Pubs

Doyle's

9 College Green. Popular with journalists from the *Irish Times*, just over the road.

The Lincoln's Inn

5 Lincoln Place. An old-style pub beside Trinity College.

Mulligan's

Poolbeg Street, behind the Screen Cinema on College Green. Escape from the tarted-up tourist venues and sip your Guinness among the smoky, green-glossed walls of this journalist's lair. A real Dublin pub.

O'Neill's

2 Suffolk Street. Tel: 679 3656. £. This atmospheric old Dublin pub is one of Dublin's best-known watering holes. It is bigger than it looks from the outside and is full of nooks and crannies. It also has the best pub carvery in the city, serving lunch from noon to 1430. Be warned that it is a favourite lunch spot with city workers, so get there before 1230 if you want to find a seat.

The Old Stand

37 Exchequer Street. Tel: 677 7220. £. Very traditional, with lots of dark mahogany. The food is traditional too: if this is to your taste try Irish Stew, or bacon and cabbage. The steaks are legendary.

Cafés and restaurants

Kilkenny Kitchen

6 Nassau Street. Tel: 677 7066. £. Open 0900–1730. Closed Sundays and public holidays. Fresh-baked scones and farmhouse cheeses complement the traditional home cooking at this pleasant restaurant, located in the Kilkenny Shop. Irish stew, casseroles, salads and an excellent house quiche.

The Runner Bean

Nassau Street. £. Situated above a vegetable shop of the same name, this is the place to come for imaginative vegetarian fare.

Tosca

20 Suffolk Street. Tel: 679 6744. £–££. Open daily 1230–1530 and 1730–midnight (Thur–Sat to 0100). Stylish but relaxed Italian restaurant serving delicious steaks and southern European-inspired food. The early-bird specials are a bargain. The owner, Norman Hewson, is the brother of U2's Bono.

Shopping

It's not surprising that some of Dublin's best bookshops can be found around Trinity College, but you'll also find a host of shops displaying a wide range of Irish crafts. Those on Nassau Street cater largely for tourists, with top-quality, traditional knitwear and gift shops, while up-and-coming artisans have studios in Pearse Street, along the north boundary of the campus.

Fred Hanna (*29 Nassau Street*) specialises in academic and Irish titles, but a good selection of posters and old postcards can also be found among the new and second-hand books. Kenny's Bookshop (*in the subterranean Trinity Square shopping mall beneath Trinity College*), is a leading supplier of Irish books, both new and second-hand, along with maps and prints, rare and antiquarian books, and gifts. The Kenny Gallery features original artwork by new Irish talent. Books Upstairs (*36 College Green*), carries gay and feminist literature and special interest titles.

The Trinity College Library Shop (*see page 45*) is a good place to find souvenirs of the *Book of Kells*, along with Irish books, Celtic-inspired jewellery, and other items.

The House of Ireland (*37–38 Nassau Street*) sells top-quality items in crystal, leather, linen, and porcelain, along with Aran knitwear and fine lambswool and cashmere sweaters. Blarney Woollen Mills (*on the corner of Nassau Street and Frederick Street South*) is the place for handwoven garments and traditional knitwear, and carries a good

selection of crystal and china. Kevin and Howlin (*31 Nassau Street*) specialises in handwoven tweed jackets and suits for men.

Contemporary ceramics, pottery, jewellery and tailored clothing by leading Irish designers is sold at the Kilkenny Shop (*5–6 Nassau Street*). Mel Bradley's handpainted silks (*Studio 61–62*) and Suzanne May's distinctive pottery (*Studio 67–68*) are produced in the Tower Design Centre in Pearse Street. You can also have jewellery made to order at the Celtic and Heraldic Jewellery Ltd (*Studio 56–58*) in the Tower Design Centre.

Celtic Note (*12 Nassau Street*) specialises in Irish music. McCullogh Piggott (*25 Suffolk Street*) sells sheet music, instruments and music books.

Try the Dublin-made Dunbarra cheese or a good selection of others at the Big Cheese Company (*Trinity Street*). The Dublin Food Co-Op (*St Andrew's Centre, Pearse Street, open Sat 1030–1700*) is Dublin's answer to a weekly farmers' market.

Illuminating thoughts

The Book of Kells, *exhibited in the Old Library at Trinity College (* see page 45 *) is acknowledged by many experts as the world's most beautiful illuminated manuscript. Kells, a small town in County Meath, northwest of Dublin, is where St Columba founded a monastery in the 6th century (* see page 149 *). Some 300 years later a group of monks from Iona, Scotland, settled at Kells after being attacked by Vikings. They are believed to be the monks who created the famous book.*

The *Book of Kells* is a copy of the four **Gospels** in Latin. Its pages measure 13in by 9in and some contain no more than a single initial letter beautifully decorated. The book was moved to Trinity College for safe keeping during the time of Cromwell.

It is not the only medieval illuminated manuscript in the care of Trinity's Old Library. The *Book of Armagh* dates from 807 and the *Book of Darrow* is even older, dating from 675, but although each of these is beautiful they lack the master touch of the monks of Kells.

Ireland was a great centre of Christian scholarship in the Middle Ages. Before the advent of printing, books were **made by hand**, and the skills of writing and book-binding were developed and preserved by **priests and monks**.

Scribes working in churches and monasteries laboriously copied religious books, especially the Bible, by hand. Philosophical and literary works from ancient Greece and Rome were also copied. The scribes eventually became authors, originating books on many aspects of Christian history and theology.

In the Middle Ages books were regarded as so important that they were decorated (**illuminated**) and treated almost as reverently as holy relics. Beautifully calligraphed, their pages were illuminated with exquisite designs and colourful scenes, often painted with real gold. The books were bound in leather which was embellished with gold, silver and precious stones.

Grafton Street

If O'Connell Street is the heart of Dublin, then the Grafton Street area is its soul. Here is the very essence of the city: busy commerce at a relaxed pace; shoppers applauding street entertainers; cafés throbbing with gossip; the ghosts of literature stalking the pubs, and, near by, the trappings of power. There's something very Celtic in this juxtaposition of politics and the raw enjoyment of life.

GRAFTON STREET

BEST OF
Grafton Street

Getting there: buses 16, 19, 22, 49, 50, 68A, 83 and 155 all pass close to the northern end of Grafton Street.

0		400m
0		400 yds

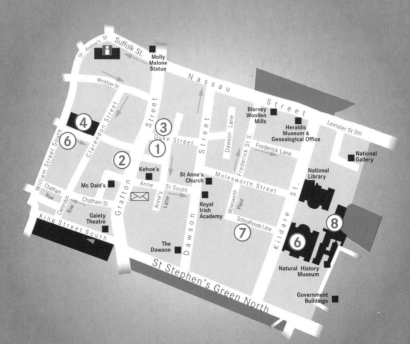

St Andrew's St · Suffolk St.

Molly Malone Statue

Wicklow St.

Nassau Street

Blarney Woollen Mills

Heraldic Museum & Genealogical Office

Leinster St Sth

National Gallery

Clarendon Street

Street

④

⑥

Duke Street

③
①

Dawson Lane

Street

Frederick St S.

Frederick Lane

William Street South

②

Kehoe's

National Library

Mc Daid's

Anne

Anne's Lane

St Anne's Church

St South

Molesworth Street

Molesworth Place

Chatham Row

Chatham St

Grafton

Royal Irish Academy

Schoolhouse Lane

Kildare St.

⑥

⑧

Clarendon Row

Gaiety Theatre

⑦

Natural History Museum

King Street South

The Dawson

Dawson

St Stephen's Green North

Government Buildings

GRAFTON STREET

① Go for gorgonzola

Follow in the footsteps of Leopold Bloom, a character from James Joyce's *Ulysses*, and drop in for a snack at Davy Byrne's pub on Duke Street. Bloom's favourite snack was a gorgonzola sandwich and a glass of burgundy. But make sure you get there early – or late – to avoid the lunchtime and post-work throng. **Page 57, 62**

② Anyone for tea?

The ground floor of Bewley's Café is where Dubliners of all ages meet to enjoy a bit of character assassination over tea and cream cakes. It's quieter upstairs among the potted palms – there's even a small museum. **Page 56**

③ Walk on the Wilde side

George Bernard Shaw, Brendan Behan, Sean O'Casey and many others of Dublin's myriad writing stars feature on the Jameson Literary Pub Crawl which starts at The Bailey, Duke Street. Actors play the literati parts on this guided tour. **Page 57**

④ Shop 'n' flop

There are two indoor shopping malls in the area, one on either side of Clarendon Street, both meeting the most demanding needs – including refreshment when cash and energy are spent. Powerscourt Townhouse Centre was originally the 18th-century home of the Powerscourt family. Use the William Street South entrance for a view of the ornamented façade. Westbury Mall is a maze of shops and cafés between Clarendon and Grafton streets. **Pages 58–59**

⑤ Curl up with a bookshop

This is the area for book-lovers. Waterstone's and Hodges Figgis on Dawson Street have large stores with a comprehensive range of titles, including sections geared to Irish literature and interests. While the International Bookshop, on Frederick Street South, has a large stock of foreign language books.

⑥ Catch up on the past

The city's tale is told in a permanent exhibition at Dublin Civic Museum, William Street South. **Page 59.** For a broader view, visit the National Museum, Kildare Street, where the collection includes Bronze Age gold ornaments, Viking artefacts, ecclesiastical treasures and exhibits dealing with Ireland's 20th-century conflicts. **Page 61**

⑦ Stare at the Mayor

Elegant Mansion House, Dawson Street, was built in 1705 and has been the official residence of the Lord Mayor of Dublin since 1715. **Page 60**

⑧ The Taoiseach!

If you're into politics, or you like to hear a good slanging match, find a Teachta Dáil (Member of Parliament) to get you into the Visitors' Gallery at Leinster House, Kildare Street. **Page 61.** You might even see the Taoiseach (Prime Minister) himself in action. **Pages 66–67**

55

Music, music, music

Dublin's heartbeat throbs to the sound of music, and nowhere more so than in Grafton Street. A stroll along the thoroughfare, pedestrianised since 1988, is like a visit to a rock and folk festival, with solo performances by traditional and classical musicians thrown in for good measure.

" *In Dublin, the definition of an introvert could be someone who has never busked on Grafton Street.* "
Dublin Tourism in *Rock 'n' Stroll*, **a guide to the city's Music Trail**

A coin tossed into a hat or fiddle case is all you're expected to pay for a gig by someone whose name may well be known worldwide the day after tomorrow. It's happened before – and more than once. Some busked on the pavement, others played in pubs.

Five of the 16 plaques along the **Rock 'n' Stroll Trail** honouring the city's musicians and singers are to be found on or very near Grafton Street. This is where some of the world's leading performers cut their teeth in public.

Bewley's Café, that hothouse of tea-table gossip, was an unlikely launch pad for the success of Bob Geldof and the Boomtown Rats. The café, as middle-class as a coffee morning, was a regular meeting place for the band and it was here that their hit single *Rat Trap* was created.

Ex-Trinity College student Chris de Burgh, whose string of successes included the world-beating *Lady in Red*, started his career in the 1970s, singing smoochy numbers to customers in **Captain America's** burger palace on Grafton Street.

Iconoclastic Christy Moore, uncompromising songwriter and solo performer and a key figure in the formation of Planxty and Moving Hearts, has his name on a plaque at Dublin's oldest theatre, the **Gaiety** on South King Street, where he's played many times since setting out on the folk circuit back in the 1960s.

The Pubs

There's no shortage of watering holes along Grafton Street, and no fear of boredom as you swig a pint of the black stuff or sip a ball o' malt (glass of whiskey). Literary figures – fact, fictitious, famous, dead or aspiring – are a feature of almost every bar.

The Bailey, 2 Duke Street, was frequented by James Joyce before he left Ireland's shores in 1912. More loyal customers have included Brendan Behan, Oliver St John Gogarty and Patrick Kavanagh. **Davy Byrne's**, across the street at No 21, owes some of its fame to the fact that Leopold Bloom, hero of Joyce's *Ulysses*, dropped by for a snack on 16 June 1904 – now celebrated annually as Bloomsday.

The Duke, 9 Duke Street, has the careworn charm of an old tweed jacket and is the haunt of cheerful but slightly world-weary bar-room philosophers and wannabe writers. You can tune in to some great conversations here.

The discreet old snugs at **Keyhoe's**, 9 South Anne Street, make eavesdropping difficult, but you can make up for it by it listening to the bar staff's laconic comments.

McDaid's, 3 Harry Street, is the quintessential Dublin pub, a fact which endeared it to its most famous client, the playwright and ex-Borstal boy Brendan Behan.

" *Grafton Street gay with housed awnings lured his senses. Muslin prints, silk, dames and dowagers, jingle of harnesses, hoofthuds lowringing in the baking causeway.* "
James Joyce,
***Ulysses*, 1922**

West of Grafton Street

The area to the west of Grafton Street is one of narrow, winding streets, tradesmen's entrances and loading bays, but among this desert of dark brick there are oases of interest. And the best way to find these is on foot.

Shopping cornucopia

The area between William Street South and Grafton Street is a cornucopia of shops and eating places. The International Bar, on the corner of St Andrew and Wicklow streets, sums up the character of the area. It's also an interesting place in its own right: a large pub with a magnificently curved wooden bar, a favourite with rock music fans and, occasionally, a venue for stand-up comedy.

There are shops selling everything from hiking gear to baby wear and musical instruments. The **Powerscourt Townhouse Centre**, best entered through the splendid façade of the mansion that once stood here on William Street South, is Dublin's most up-market shopping mall. Richard, third Viscount Powerscourt, for whom the mansion was completed in 1774, would probably not be dismayed by the quality of the jewellery, crafts and fashion available through the centre's 80 shops.

At the opposite end of the scale, nearby **George's Arcade**, a covered market reaching across to South Great George's Street, presents everything from fruit and vegetables to second-hand clothing and books, collectables and antiques.

Dublin Civic Museum

58 William Street South. Tel: 679 4260. Tue–Sat 1000–1800, Sun 1100–1400. Free.

The most curious exhibit in this museum, which is opposite the Powerscourt Townhouse Centre on William Street South, is the head of Admiral Lord Horatio Nelson, the 19th-century British naval hero – in stone, that is. The Admiral in his entirety used to stand atop a column in O'Connell Street. The monument was erected by the British in 1808 and destroyed in an IRA explosion in 1966 (*see page 27*).

Other exhibits in the museum tell the city's story through artefacts and memorabilia, including a map of 1728 and a set of aquatints of 1793 which together display Dublin at its Georgian peak.

The building housing the museum is Georgian. In 1765 it housed the Society of Artists and became home to the City Assembly in 1791.

Monkey business

Carved figures at the foot of the columns outside the Heraldic Museum in Kildare Street depict monkeys playing billiards. The building originally housed the Kildare Street Club, founded in 1782, and the slyly humorous carvings are the work of sculptor Charles Harrison.

GRAFTON STREET

East of Grafton Street

Here you will find the official residence of the Lord Mayor of Dublin and elegant St Anne's Church. Kildare Street has Leinster House, home of the Dáil, the Irish Parliament, as well as the National Museum, the National Library, and the one-time home of Bram Stoker, creator of Count Dracula (No 30 Kildare Steet).

Mansion House

The area was developed in 1705 by Joshua Dawson, and within two years the wide boulevard named after him was considered to be Dublin's finest street. Dawson's next project was to build himself a grand home, but this was still unfinished when the city corporation offered to buy it as a residence for the Lord Mayor. The price agreed was £3500, with a ground rent to be paid each Christmas of 40 shillings and a 6lb loaf of double refined sugar. Thus Dublin acquired a Mansion House for its Lord Mayor before London had one. It's not usually open to the public.

St Anne's Church

St Anne's Church dates from 1720, but its present façade was erected in 1868 when the church was rebuilt by architects Deane and Woodward. In 1723 Lord Newtown left a bequest to the church to buy bread for the poor. The tradition continues today and the bread is distributed from a special shelf erected beside the altar.

Leinster House

Members of the public are only admitted to Leinster House in Kildare Street, through an introduction by a member of the Dáil (*see pages 66–67*). However, the exterior of the building can be viewed from the ornate main gates and from the rotundas on either side which now house the **National Museum** and the **National Library** respectively. (*see below*).

National Museum

Kildare Street. Tel: 677 7444. Tue–Sat 1000–1700, Sun 1400–1700. Free. Guided tours when available, £.

The National Museum, on the south side of Leinster House, houses Celtic antiquities, artefacts from the Iron and Bronze Ages and a wide range of Viking items excavated from sites in Dublin. The Treasury is a permanent exhibition of early Irish art, including a stunning collection of Bronze Age jewellery and the Ardagh and Derrynaflan chalices, the Tara Brooch, the Cross of Cong and St Patrick's Bell. The Road to Independence is a section of the museum devoted to Ireland's tumultuous political history during the first quarter of the 20th century.

National Library

Kildare Street. Tel: 661 8811. Mon 1000–2100, Tue–Wed, Thur–Fri 1000–1700, Sat 1000–1300. Free.

Exhibitions drawn from the National Museum's massive collection of books, magazines, newspapers, maps, photographs and manuscripts are mounted in the entrance hall of the National Library, which occupies the rotunda on the north side of Leinster House. The collection was originally built up by the Royal Dublin Society, which once owned all three buildings.

Eating and drinking

Relaxing with friends and having fun are food and drink to the Irish, and nowhere more so than in Dublin. Grafton Street and environs, the city's good-time centre, is well served by places for eating, drinking and merry-making. Remember, however, that by some standards Dublin is not a late-night city. Even the most sophisticated restaurants bring the shutters down by 2330 and the wildest clubs close at 0230. For the area's best pubs see page 57.

Cafés and restaurants

The Chilli Club

1 Anne's Lane. Tel: 677 4721. £–££. Authentic Thai cuisine in a warm and friendly setting. *Lunch Mon–Sat, dinner daily.*

Cooke's Café

14 William Street South. Tel: 679 0536. ££. The style is new age in this restaurant which serves Mediterranean, Californian and seafood dishes. *Lunch and dinner daily.*

Davy Byrne's

21 Duke Street. Tel: 677 5217. ££. The pub immortalised in James Joyce's *Ulysses* is also a restaurant renowned for its seafood and traditional Irish dishes. *Lunch and dinner daily.*

Fitzers

51 Dawson Street. Tel: 677 1155. £–££. Given the right weather at the right time of year, you can eat *al fresco* at this fashionable establishment.

Californian and Italian dishes are served, with the emphasis on seafood. *Daily 0900–2330.*

La Cave

28 Anne Street South. Tel: 679 4409. £–££. Carnivores and vegetarians can find satisfaction in the city's oldest French wine bar. *Daily 1230–2300.*

Le Caprice

12 St Andrew Street. Tel: 679 4050. £££. A pianist plays as diners enjoy what many regard as the finest Italian fare in Dublin. Dublin Bay provides fresh supplies of seafood daily. *Tue–Sat 1800–0015.*

Marrakesh Restaurant

1st Floor, 28 Anne Street South. Tel: 670 5255. ££. Couscous, mechoui and other exotic Moroccan dishes served in authentic surroundings. *Daily 1800–2330.*

Peacock Alley

47 William Street South. Tel: 662 0760.
££–£££. The style is Mediterranean
served with the panache of an Irish
chef whose talent was honed in the
competitive kitchens of New York.
Conrad Gallagher's restaurant is the
city's most prestigious. *Lunch and*
dinner daily.

Periwinkle Seafood Bar

Powerscourt Townhouse Centre.
Tel: 679 4203. £–££. Reasonably
priced quality seafood in a Bord
Fáilte award-winning establishment.
Mon–Sat 1130–1700.

Rajdoot Tandoori

26–28 Clarendon Street. Tel: 679
4274. £–££. Traditional North Indian
cuisine, with excellent vegetarian
dishes. *Lunch and dinner Mon–Sat.*

Royal Garden

Westbury Centre. Tel: 679 1397. £–££.
This was the first Chinese restaurant
in the city to win a Bord Fáilte award
of excellence. *Lunch and dinner*
Mon–Fri; Sat–Sun 1230–midnight.

Clubs and nightlife

Da Club

2 Johnson's Place, off Clarendon Row.
Tel: 670 5116. Entrance fee. Stand-up
comedy, live music and witty DJs. 'Da'
is short for Dublin Arts. *Mon–Sat*
2230–0200.

Gaiety Theatre

King Street South. Tel: 677 1717.
Entrance fee. Cabaret, jazz and rock
groups keep the action going in three
bars, and there's a disco, too. *Fri–Sat*
2300–0230.

Lillie's Bordello

Adam Court, Grafton Street.
Tel: 679 9204. Entrance fee (£ Sun
and Mon). Not half as risqué as it
sounds, but a fun place nonetheless.
Daily 2300–0230.

Shopping

Almost everything you could want – at whatever price you're prepared to pay – is available in the Grafton Street area. As well as Powerscourt Townhouse Centre and Westbury Mall (see pages 55 and 58–59), there are plenty of other places large and small to tempt your credit card to the limit.

Pedestrianised Grafton Street itself has an eclectic range of shops and is a great place for drifting and window-shopping without the need for matador-like traffic-dodging. The leading department stores here are **Brown Thomas**, up-market without being stand-offish, and neighbouring **Marks & Spencer**, the British middle-class shopping institution.

If you're simply looking for something as expressive or as emotional as a bunch of flowers you'll be spoilt for choice – stallholders with gorgeously colourful displays of blooms are located along the length of the street.

The labyrinth of arcades, alleys and narrow streets lying between Grafton Street and Dawson Street is the place for impulse buying of anything from antiquarian maps to buttons, coins and jewellery. Between Dawson and Kildare streets, along Molesworth Street, Frederick Street South and Kildare Street itself, are a number of women's fashion boutiques, art galleries and craft and antiques shops.

For men's and women's designer clothing look out along Anne Street South and Duke Street – have your gold card at the ready – or try **The Design Centre** in Powerscourt Townhouse Centre or the aforementioned Brown Thomas. The **Royal Hibernian Way**, a small shopping mall in Dawson Street with some very exclusive clothing shops, is also worth seeking out.

Those on a mid-range fashion budget will find many of their favourite stores in the area. **Airwave**, **Benetton**, **Miss Selfridge**, **Monsoon**, **Next**, **Principles** and **River Island** can all be found on Grafton Street.

Jewellery shops are dotted all over the area. Start your search in Johnson's Court, alongside Bewley's. Here you'll find something for all tastes and budgets. And for those who don't have to think about a budget, there's **Appleby's**. Modern Irish creations are on display – and on sale – at the **Crafts Council of Ireland** section of the Powerscourt Townhouse Centre.

For distinctive knitwear try **Cleo Ltd** (*18 Kildare Street*). They only use natural fibres for their handknitted sweaters and accessories, made to their own designs. **Monaghan's** (*Grafton Arcade*) is the place for cashmere. For Irish linen goods make your way to **Needlecraft**, 27 Dawson Street, where you will also find everything you need to engage in knitting, crochet or embroidery.

Music-lovers are well served. **HMV** has a three-storey record emporium and ticket agency at 65 Grafton Street, while the ubiquitous **Tower Records**, complete with a special section selling books and magazines, can be found at 16 Wicklow Street. **Golden Discs**, Ireland's largest chain of music stores, has a branch on Grafton Street, next to the Grafton Arcade. **Celtic Note**, 12 Nassau Street, specialises in Irish music. If you're looking for second-hand bargains on cassette or disc seek out **Borderline**, Duke's Lane.

Tracing your ancestors

Anyone with an interest in heraldry will find information on the uses of coats of arms, shields, banners, seals, old coins and all matters appertaining to the subject at the Heraldic Museum. It is the only museum of its kind in the world, and is housed in the office of the Chief Herald at 2 Kildare Street; tel: 677-7444. It is free, and open Mon–Fri 1030–1630. The National Genealogical Office in the same building is where people can trace their Irish ancestry.

Ireland's top talkers

From the street, which is the closest most visitors can get without an invitation from a member of the Dáil, Leinster House looks more like an art gallery than the powerhouse of Irish politics – a symbolic notion, perhaps, since the Irish, more than anyone, have turned the hurly-burly of debate on any subject into an art form.

This is where the big issues of Irish life are mauled, if not settled, by 226 people. Politics in Ireland – whether national or international – can be entertaining, dramatic, historic, but never dull.

The Republic of Ireland is governed as a parliamentary democracy with an upper and lower chamber – the **Dáil (House of Representatives)** and the **Seanad (Senate)**. The President is head of state and the Taoiseach (Prime Minister) is head of the government. Unless only one candidate is put forward, the President is elected by direct popular vote.

Ireland's constitution was adopted by referendum in 1937. It defines the powers of government, the President and Prime Minister, as well as the structure and powers of the courts, and sets out the fundamental rights of citizens.

GRAFTON STREET

The President is also the supreme commander of the country's defence forces. There is no Vice-President. If the President dies or is incapacitated the constitution provides for a commission to act in his or her place. The commission would consist of the Chief Justice and the chairmen of the Dáil and Seanad.

The **Taoiseach** is appointed by the President on nomination of the Dáil and must resign if he or she ceases to retain the support of the majority in the Dáil.

The Dáil has 166 members, known as Teachta' Dáil (TDs), with six main political parties represented: Fianna Fáil, Fine Gail, Labour, Progressive Democrats, Democratic Left and the Green Party. TDs are elected by proportional representation. The Seanad, with 60 members, may initiate or amend legislation, but in the case of financial bills may make recommendations only.

Before signing a bill, the President may ask the **Supreme Court** to decide its compatibility with the Constitution, a procedure which has led to a number of laws or parts of laws being declared void. All citizens have the right to petition the courts to secure their rights or to have a judgment pronounced as to whether or not given legislation is constitutional.

Local government in Ireland is responsible for public housing, water and sanitation, road maintenance, vocational education and other services. It is administered by 113 local authorities and services are funded by state grants and local taxes.

Georgian Dublin

Dublin's heyday in architecture and town planning
was in the 18th and 19th centuries and the city is
bejewelled with fine Georgian buildings. The
pinnacle of residential development was achieved
south of the River Liffey, around Merrion Square and
St Stephen's Green, two spacious areas of public
parkland still surrounded by splendid buildings.

GEORGIAN DUBLIN

BEST OF

Georgian Dublin

Getting there: buses 10, 11, 13, 14, 44, 46A and 47 all serve St Stephen's Green.

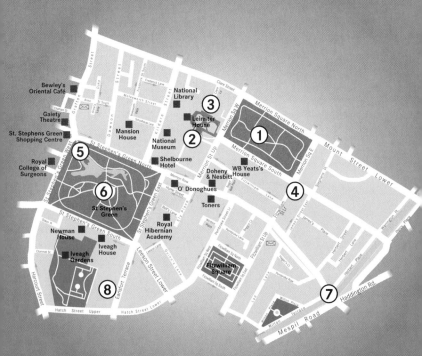

① Scores of doors

Take your camera and a couple of rolls of film when you stroll along Merrion Square and the surrounding streets and take some of those classic poster shots you will see everywhere.
Pages 72–73

② The dead zoo

Characteristically dismissive, Dubliners call the Natural History Museum on Merrion Street 'the dead zoo'. True, it's a museum in the old Victorian style, but it's full of fascinating stuffed animals, skeletons and strange things suspended in glass jars. **Page 73**

③ In the frame

More than 2000 works, including paintings by Jack B Yeats, brother of the poet W B Yeats, are on show in the National Gallery of Ireland, Merrion Square West. Acclaimed as one of Europe's best small art museums, it has collections representing every major European school of painting, though the emphasis is on Irish portraits and landscapes. **Page 73**

④ 29 on the line

See how middle-class Dubliners lived between 1790 and 1820. The number in question is 29 Lower Fitzwilliam Street, a house which has been totally restored, refurbished and frozen in time. **Page 73**

⑤ A ride on the side

Take a horse-drawn carriage ride from Fusiliers' Arch at the northwest corner of St Stephen's Green and see the sights from a different angle.

⑥ Be seen on the Green

Given the right weather, this is where workers and visitors to the city centre bring their sandwiches and soak up the sun. Take a look at the many sculptures on the Green – everyone from Wolfe Tone to Lord Ardilaun, even old Arthur Guinness himself, is represented. **Pages 74–75**

⑦ By the old canal…

If you call at the tourism information centre near Baggot Street Bridge, find time for a stroll along the towpath of the Grand Canal, a tranquil waterway that starts less than a mile to the east, and continues westwards for about 100 miles. You don't have to walk that far, however, to appreciate the historic canal's beauty. **Pages 82–83**

⑧ Face the music

If you are a music-lover, it's worth checking out to see what's on at the National Concert Hall. The emphasis is on classical music and opera, but pop concerts are staged from time to time.
Page 78

Merrion Square

The square was laid out in 1752 by John Ensor for the second Viscount Fitzwilliam of Merrion, who wanted to lure Dublin's uppercrust families to the south side of the river. The original houses are still standing, and handsome they are, too, with their ornate front doors and fanlights, brass knockers and intricate wrought-iron balconies.

Today, many of the houses serve as offices for companies and institutions. Among these are the Irish Architectural Archive, the Royal Society of Antiquaries in Ireland and the Catholic Central Library which houses some 60,000 books, newspapers and magazines. The Irish Traditional Music Archive, on the south side of the square, has a comprehensive collection of sound recordings, books and manuscripts.

A quieter alternative to St Stephen's Green for picnics, the park in the centre of the square is attractively laid out with shrubs and flower beds and features a number of sculptures. Among them is a bust of Henry Grattan by Peter Grant and the figure of Éire by Jerome Connor. Tribute Head, by Dame Elizabeth Frink, was unveiled on South Africa Freedom Day in June 1983 to mark Nelson Mandela's 20th year of imprisonment. It was donated by Artists for Amnesty.

Number 29

29 Lower Fitzwilliam Street. Tel: 702 6155. Tue–Sat 1000–1700, Sun 1400–1700. Admission: £; concessions.

To see how well-heeled Dubliners lived in the late 18th and early 19th centuries, stroll round to the southeast corner of the square and call in on the house they call Number 29. The house was restored after a public outcry at the destruction in the 1960s of 20 nearby Georgian structures to make way for a new headquarters for the Electricity Supply Board. It was furnished and decorated by the National Museum.

Natural History Museum

Merrion Street. Tel: 677 7444. Tue–Sat 1000–1700, Sun 1400–1700. Free.

The Natural History Museum, at the southwest corner of the square, is one of those splendidly old-fashioned museums with a creepy, slightly Gothic ambience. Dubliners call it 'the dead zoo', but it's informative and fun for all that. Here you'll find the skeletons of huge deer, popularly known as Irish elk, and those of whales stranded on Irish beaches. There are buffalo and deer and exhibits of Irish wildlife, and jars filled with things that once wriggled, slithered or squirmed.

National Gallery of Ireland

Merrion Square West. Tel: 661 5133. Mon–Wed and Fri–Sat 1000–1715, Thur 1000–2030, Sun 1400–1700. Free.

The institutional 19th-century façade to the National Gallery of Ireland belies the treasure house within. The collections embrace the 14th to the 20th centuries, including works by Degas, El Greco, Goya, Monet and Picasso – among other great names – to say nothing of Irish painters. One room is devoted to works by Jack B Yeats. Many, however, consider the *pièce de résistance* to be Caravaggio's *The Taking of Christ*, discovered in 1992 in the Dublin Jesuit House of Study.

St Stephen's Green

Dublin's largest square – a quarter of a mile in each direction and covering 22 acres – St Stephen's Green was a tract of rough common ground until 1664 when the city corporation set it aside as an open space for the use of citizens. The land was ploughed, levelled, planted with trees and enclosed by a stone wall. The trouble was no one could get there.

Access from the city to the new park was along a rough lane which was 'so foule and out of repaire that persons cannot passe'. In 1671 the corporation ordered that the lane should be put in order, and pedestrians have been using Grafton Street as the main route to St Stephen's Green ever since.

With good access, the green became very popular and by the 18th century the north side was a fashionable promenade known as Beaux' Walk. Today, some of Dublin's most exclusive gentlemen's clubs are to be found in this stretch. Here, too, is the eminent **Shelbourne Hotel** (*see pages 76–77*).

In 1814 the city father's decided that the green was too good for the hoi-polloi. The square was enclosed within railings and locked gates and the only people allowed in were local residents who paid a guinea a year for the privilege.

In 1877 Sir Arthur Guinness, later Lord Ardilaun, came to the rescue of the common citizen. As MP for the city, he pushed through an Act of Parliament which reopened the green to the public. Then he personally funded its present layout and the park was opened in 1880. Twelve years later a grateful city erected a statue of him which you can see today on the west side of the green.

The green is dotted with monuments. The first thing you see as you leave Grafton Street is Fusiliers' Arch, a massive structure commemorating soldiers of the Dublin Fusiliers who served in the Anglo-Boer War. Among others, there are busts of the poet James Mangan, the feminist nationalist Countess Constance Markievicz, and James Joyce, a statue of Irish nationalist Robert Emmet, a memorial by Henry Moore dedicated to W B Yeats and the huge monument to Wolfe Tone which Dubliners know as 'Tonehenge'.

The green also contains a lake, a bandstand where free concerts are staged in the summer and a fountain depicting the _Three Fates_, a gift from Germany in appreciation of Ireland's relief aid after World War II.

Newman House

85–86 St Stephen's Green. Tel: 706 7422.
Guided tours Tue–Fri 1200–1600, Sat 1400–1600;
June–Aug Sun 1100–1200.

On the quieter south side of the square stands Newman House, where the Catholic University of Ireland was opened in 1853. Completed in 1765, the building is named after the university's first Rector, the English theologian John Henry Newman. The university is now incorporated with University College, Dublin, and among its most illustrious graduates are Padraig Pearse, a leader of the 1916 Rising, President Eamon de Valera and James Joyce. The English poet Gerard Manly Hopkins, who died of typhoid in Dublin, was Professor of Classics here. The house is noted for its rococo stucco work and 19th-century furniture.

The Shelbourne

On the northwest edge of St Stephen's Green, the Shelbourne Hotel is said to be 'the most distinguished address in Ireland'. The entrance alone, adorned by the figures of Nubian maidens and their slaves, to say nothing of the top-hatted doorman, marks it as one of the world's grandest hotels.

The Shelbourne first opened its doors as a modest town hotel in 1824, but its location on the fashionable north side of the green soon attracted the rich and the famous. Among the earliest of a line of celebrities was William Makepeace Thackeray who paid six shillings and eight pence for full board in 1842 and included a drawing of his hotel window in his *Irish Sketch Book*.

Later writers who stayed there could not help writing about the place. George Moore and Oliver St Gogarty succumbed, while Elizabeth Bowen was so taken with it that she wrote a 200-page book. James Joyce never stayed at the Shelbourne, but he still included it in one of his *Dubliners* short stories, and in *Ulysses*.

Grandstand views

During the 1916 Rising, guests found they had a front row view of the action as rebel forces, led by the pistol-packing Countess Markievicz, fought against British troops on St Stephen's Green. As the fighting intensified and bullets ricocheted off the hotel's façade, staff led the guests to a back room to continue their afternoon tea.

In 1922 the Constitution of the Irish Free State was drafted in the Shelbourne, and the hotel was once more at the hub of the action when civil war broke out.

You don't have to stay at the Shelbourne to enjoy some of the facilities of the country's most fashionable address. Wander into the lobby to admire the splendid chandelier, drink a pint of Guinness in the bar or take morning coffee or afternoon tea in the Lord Mayor's Lounge.

" *If a man is born in a stable, it doesn't mean he is a horse.* "

The Duke of Wellington, who was born in Dublin but didn't want to be considered Irish

South of the green
Iveagh House and Gardens

One of the most impressive buildings on the south side of St Stephen's Green is Iveagh House, once a Guinness family home and now headquarters of the Irish government's Department of Foreign Affairs.

Built in 1763 as a mansion for the Bishop of Cork and Ross, it was acquired in 1856 by Benjamin Lee Guinness, Arthur's father, who also bought the house next door and merged the two. The second Earl of Iveagh gave the house to the nation in 1939. Imposing enough from the outside, the building has a magnificent interior, but unfortunately is not open to the public.

Iveagh Gardens, behind the house *are* open to the public – a fact which is not widely known, even among Dubliners. The gardens, an oasis of quiet for those in the know, are reached from behind the **National Concert Hall** in Earlsfort Terrace or through a gate in Clonmel Street, off Harcourt Road. The National Concert Hall (now the city's main venue for classical concerts) was completed in 1865 as the central hall for the Dublin International Exhibition that year and was later incorporated as the Great Hall of **University College Dublin**.

UCD, the second best-known of Dublin's academic triumvirate (the third is Dublin City University), has long since moved to Belfield, among the outer suburbs to the south, but part of the faculty of engineering remains at Earlsfort Terrace. The courtyard of the neighbouring **Conrad Hotel** contains a fountain with a striking group of bronze birds and a plaque quoting the line, 'For peace comes dropping slow,' from W B Yeats's poem *Lake Isle of Inisfree*.

Shaw's Birthplace

33 Synge Street. Tel: 475 0845. May–Oct Mon–Sat 1000–1700, Sun and public holidays 1100–1700. Admission: £; concessions.

At No 1 Hatch Street Lower, which intersects about halfway down Earlsfort Terrace, the youthful George Bernard Shaw lived with his mother and her singing teacher, George Vandeleur Lee, who had invited the Shaws to stay with him. Shaw's Birthplace, near by, is now a museum. The neat terraced house has been restored, looking as though the family had just stepped out for a while. Visitors can see the drawing-room where Mrs Shaw held musical evenings, the parlour and the children's bedrooms. The house gives an insight into domestic life in Victorian Dublin, as well as the early years of a Nobel Prize-winning playwright.

Irish Jewish Museum

3–4 Walworth Road, Portobello. Tel: 453 1797. May–Sept Sun, Tue, Thur 1100–1530; Oct–Apr Sun only 1030–1430 or by appointment. Donation.

Synge Street stands on the edge of what used to be Dublin's Jewish quarter and a former synagogue near by is now the Irish Jewish Museum. A reconstructed kitchen is typical of a Jewish home in the area at end of the 19th century, and there is a collection of documents, artefacts and memorabilia. The museum was opened in 1985 by the son of the first Chief Rabbi of Ireland, Dr Chaim Herzog, President of Israel.

The vaults of an old railway station at the corner of Hatch Street Upper and Harcourt Street now house one of Dublin's best-known nightclubs – PoD (Place of Dance) – and Findlaters wine merchants whose cellars include a small museum which is freely open to the public.

Just a few minutes' walk south of Harcourt Street, Portobello Bridge crosses the Grand Canal (see pages 82–83).

Cafés and restaurants

Ayumi-Ya

132 Lower Baggot Street. Tel: 662 0233. £. Informal, inexpensive eating in Ireland's first Japanese restaurant, established in 1983. *Lunch and dinner daily.*

The Commons

85–86 St Stephen's Green. Tel: 475 2597. £££. The setting is one of Dublin's finest Georgian town houses, the ambience tranquil and elegant, the cuisine inspired and modern. *Lunch Mon–Fri, dinner Mon–Sat.*

Dobbins

15 Stephen's Lane. Tel: 676 4679. A favourite with Dublin journalists and politicians, this is a fun eating place with a welcoming and attentive staff, led by their congenial boss, John O'Byrne. *Lunch Mon–Fri, dinner Tue–Sat.*

FXB's

1A Lower Pembroke Street, off Baggot Street. Tel: 676 4606. ££. One of a small local chain specialising in steaks, and doing it well. *Lunch Mon–Fri, dinner Mon–Sat.*

The Grey Door

22–23 Upper Pembroke Street. Tel: 676 3286. ££–£££. Imagine a combination of Irish, Scandinavian and Russian dishes and you have the Grey Door's menu. *Lunch Mon–Fri, dinner Mon–Sat.*

Il Posto

10 St Stephen's Green. Tel: 679 4769. ££. Authentic Italian cuisine in simple but comfortable surroundings. *Lunch and dinner daily.*

Latchford's Bistro

100 Lower Baggot Street. Tel: 676 0784. ££. French/international cuisine with the emphasis on Irish steaks and fresh seafood. *Lunch Mon–Fri, dinner Mon–Sat.*

Pier 23

23 Upper Pembroke Street. Tel: 676 1494. ££. Dishes from throughout Ireland are presented in an old-world setting with pine furnishings and open fires. *Lunch Mon–Fri, dinner daily.*

Restaurant Patrick Guilbaud

21 Upper Merrion Street. Tel: 676 4192. £££. Dubliners know it simply as 'RPG', where the best of Irish produce becomes the best of French cuisine. *Lunch and dinner Tue–Sat.*

The Unicorn

12B Merrion Court, Merrion Row. Tel: 668 8552. ££–£££. All-day Italian dishes in a well-established and very popular café-restaurant. *Open from 0900 daily; piano bar Wed–Sat 2100–0300.*

Pubs and clubs

Doheny and Nesbitt

5 Lower Baggot Street. Tel: 676 2945.
It sounds more like a firm of solicitors
than a pub, and in fact many of its
clients are lawyers, but it's a jolly
place for all that, and a Dublin classic.

O'Donoghue's

15 Merrion Row. Tel: 660 7194. The
pub's reputation for putting on good
Irish music began with The Dubliners,
and continues with today's up-and-
coming performers.

Toner's

*139 Lower Baggot Street. Tel: 676
3090. Archetypal Dublin pub – a
place for informal chat and serious
eavesdropping.*

PoD

*Corner of Hatch Street, Harcourt
Street. Tel: 478 0225. Entrance fee.*
The city's stylish 'Place of Dance'.
Wed–Sun 2300–0230. Upstairs is the
noisier, more adolescent **Red Box**.
Thur–Sat 2200–0230. Entrance fee.

Shopping

This is not Dublin's best area for shopping, but there is a wide range of shops –
including a branch of **Dunne's** – ranged on three floors around a central atrium
in the spacious **St Stephen's Centre** at the northwest corner of St Stephen's
Green. Here, you can buy anything from a birthday card to a Donegal tweed
jacket, and there's an excellent cafeteria and good parking to boot.

81

Jones's Delicatessen, 137 Baggot Street Lower, sells all the makings for a
picnic in any of the area's parks or on the canalside.

Ulysses – the soap

*Sweeney's Pharmacy in Lincoln Place, near the intersection with Merrion
Street Lower, is where Leopold Bloom bought a bar of lemon soap in
Chapter 5 of James Joyce's* Ulysses. *The shop has survived much as it
was in 1904 and, yes, you can still buy the lemon soap.*

Dublin's canals

The area fronting the Grand Canal to the right of Portobello Bridge is known to this day as Portobello Harbour, although it has not been used as a harbour since the 1940s, when many of the wharves and docks were filled in. Portobello House, the elegant brick building with the colonnaded portico, clock and cupola, now housing the Institute of Education, was originally a hotel, one of five built between Dublin and the River Shannon to accommodate passengers travelling on horse-drawn barges.

The canal was built between 1755 and 1796 to carry passengers and freight between Dublin and Shannon Harbour, a distance of about 100 miles, and the Portobello Hotel opened in July 1807. Passenger traffic came to an end in 1852, but the hotel remained in business for another eight years when it became a convent hospital for blind women. Later, it served as a private nursing home and hospice – Jack B Yeats, the poet's artist brother, spent his last years here.

Dublin's hinterland was connected by the **Grand Canal** to much of Ireland, thanks to the **River Shannon**, and contains the largest area of inland waters in the British Isles. Waterways at the northern end of the river made it possible for goods to be shifted from Dublin to Belfast without negotiating rough roads or stormy seas.

The Grand's success prompted the opening of a second canal, the **Royal**, which was completed in 1817, taking a line to the Shannon through the northern outskirts of Dublin. The new waterway, however, was never a serious contender to the well-established Grand, and the coming of the railways sent both canals into decline.

The last commercial craft sailed on the Grand Canal in 1960 and the **Royal** closed completely a year later. The Grand, however, continued to be used as a leisure waterway by boaters, walkers, anglers and nature lovers. Its towpath provided a favourite walk for the poet **Patrick Kavanagh**, who is commemorated by an evocative statue near **Baggot Street Bridge**.

The Grand Canal links with the River Barrow, as well as the Shannon, providing a boating – and walking and cycling – route through southeast Ireland as far as Waterford. At the northern end of the Shannon, the recently restored **Shannon-Erne Waterway** extends cruising from Leitrim through Northern Ireland to Belleek, less than 10 miles from Co Donegal's Atlantic shores. These two links provide Ireland with the most extensive dedicated leisure cruising area in Europe – a total distance of some 500 miles.

Restoration work is now being carried out on the Royal Canal and there are plans to reopen the defunct Ulster Canal, which will re-forge the old link between Dublin and Belfast.

To find out about Ireland's waterways, call at the **Waterways Visitor Centre** (*Grand Canal Quay, Pearse Street; tel: 677 7510; June–Sept daily 0930–1830; Oct–May Wed–Sun 1230–1700; admission: £; concessions*). Seemingly floating in the old canal basin, the centre portrays the historical and ecological story of Ireland's rivers, loughs and canals.

Old Dublin

Old Dublin arose from a primitive settlement at a point where three rivers met and evolved with each new group of traders and invaders. Celtic missionaries, Vikings, Normans, the English – each piled new buildings and cultural influences on top of the old. The result is a fascinating mish-mash of old streets, two cathedrals and a castle in an area where the past cries from every stone.

85

BEST OF
Old Dublin

Getting there: buses 49, 50, 54A, 68A and 123 pass close to Wood Quay, Christ Church Cathedral and Dublin Castle.

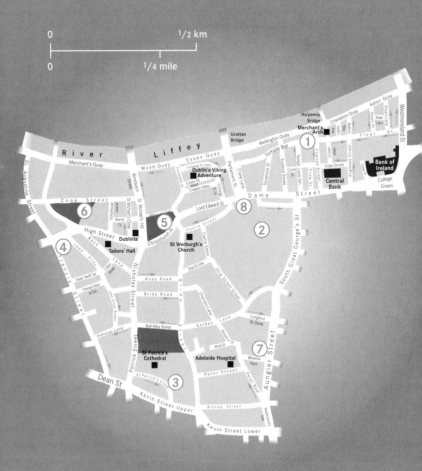

River Liffey

Merchant's Quay · Wood Quay · Essex Quay · Wellington Quay · Grattan Bridge · Temple Bar · Ha'penny Bridge · Merchant's Arch · Crampton Quay · Aston Quay · Fleet St · Westmoreland St

Bank of Ireland · College Green

Central Bank · Dame Street

Dublin's Viking Adventure

Cook Street · High Street · Dublinia · Tailors' Hall · St Werburgh's Church · Lord Edward St · Christchurch Pl · Castle Street

Ross Road · Bride Road · Golden Lane · Bull Alley Street · St Patrick's Cathedral · Adelaide Hospital · Peter Street

Dean St · St Patrick's Close · Kevin Street Upper · Bishop Street · Kevin Street Lower

Aungier Street · South Great George's St

① ② ③ ④ ⑤ ⑥ ⑦ ⑧

OLD DUBLIN

① Temple Bar

Temple Bar might well have become a bus station if the council's plans had not been resisted, Instead it is Dublin's Left Bank, the place where young Dubliners and visitors come for food, music and fun. **Pages 88-89**

② Tour the towers

Dublin Castle has changed a lot since a defensive earthwork was built here even before the Vikings arrived in 841, and although it doesn't look much like a castle today, it's still well worth a visit. **Pages 96-97**

③ Caged in

Marsh's Library was the first public library in Ireland when it opened in 1701. The interior, unchanged since it was built, contains three wired cages into which readers were locked with valuable books. **Page 99**

④ The Liberties

The area west of Francis Street lay beyond the city walls in medieval times and was free from the general restrictions on trade and other matters. For generations it had a reputation for lawlessness, and though it still isn't entirely squeaky clean, it's a great place for antiques and second-hand bargains. **Pages 100-101**

⑤ Strongbow, weak roof

Christ Church Cathedral contains the tomb of Strongbow, Earl of Pembroke, who invaded Dublin in 1170. Business deals were settled over the tomb until 1562 when the cathedral roof collapsed, destroying the tomb. The effigy of an unknown knight was brought in so the deals could continue. **Pages 92-93**

⑥ Get lucky

Touch the 'Lucky Stone', an early Christian gravestone in the porch of St Audoen's Church of Ireland church, and … who knows? The church is one of the city's oldest, with a 12th-century tower and font and a 15th-century nave. **Page 99**

⑦ Relics of a saint

Why not pledge your troth in Whitefriar Street Carmelite Church, where a casket contains the remains of Valentine, the patron saint of love? **Page 99**

⑧ City motto

A mosaic in the entrance rotunda of the impressive City Hall shows the Corporation's coat of arms with the motto, *Obedientia Civium Urbis Felicitas* (Happy the city where citizens obey). **Page 98**

A maze of fun

Some people come to Dublin and spend the whole time in Temple Bar. Unfortunately, these have sometimes been stag party groups over from Britain and other parts of Europe and their behaviour hasn't always been decorous. But the Irish have had enough. 'Craic' is fun – hooliganism is not. Troublemakers now can expect to make a sudden and unceremonious exit from Temple Bar, and if they're from another country out of Ireland altogether.

That said, Temple Bar *is* a place for fun. Its narrow old streets, laid out in the 18th century and now mostly pedestrianised, are a maze of bistros, boutiques, cafés, ethnic restaurants, pubs and art galleries, many of which have frontages decorated with vivid murals. It is home to a number of cultural centres, and there's always something going on – jazz and rock festivals, art exhibitions, open-air theatre.

Temple Bar lies south of the river between Grattan and O'Connell Bridges and stretches back to Dame Street. You can reach it from any side turning on the north side of Dame Street, but the best way is to cross Ha'penny Bridge from the opposite side of the Liffey and enter the district through Merchants' Arch. This gives the keenest experience of the medieval bazaar ambience that pervades Temple Bar.

Culturally, there's something for everyone.

The Ark Children's Cultural Centre
(*11A Eustace Street; tel: 670 7788; Tue–Fri 0930–1600, Sat 1000–1600; admission: ££*) is an arts centre for children aged 4 to 14. It has a theatre, workshop and gallery.

The Irish Film Centre (*6 Eustace Street; tel: 679 3477; weekly and annual membership*) is a spacious 18th-century warehouse converted into a centre with two screens, an archive section and a restaurant/bar. There is a continuing programme of Irish and European arthouse films and lectures and seminars are held frequently.

The Olympia Theatre (*74 Dame Street; tel: 677 7744*) is Dublin's oldest surviving music-hall. It opened in 1870 and now offers a wide range of entertainment and drama, but is best known for its midnight shows and gigs.

Temple Bar Gallery and Studios (*5–9 Temple Bar; tel: 671 0073; Mon–Sat 1000–1800, Sun 1400–1800; free*), a former factory, has been converted to provide exhibition space and working studios for 30 professional artists in all media, including painting, sculpture and photography.

Temple Bar Music Centre (*Curved Street; tel: 764 9202; opening times vary; admission: ££*) provides combined recording studios for sound and television and a venue for seated audience and dancing gigs. Music offered ranges from traditional Irish to the wildest in contemporary sound.

The best known of Temple Bar's clubs – and reputed to be the best in the city – is **Kitchen** (*East Essex Street; tel: 677 6635; daily 2330–0230; admission: ££*), owned by the band U2. The main dance floor is surrounded by a moat!

To find out what's going on in the area call at the **Temple Bar Information Centre** (*18 Eustace Street; tel: 671 5717*), opposite The Ark (*see page 88*).

Viking adventure

Dublin wasn't much more than a hamlet when the Vikings arrived in 841. The newcomers lost no time in building fortifications and a harbour, then set about pillaging other parts of Ireland, using their new colony as a base.

Compared with the Irish, who until now had been enjoying their 'golden age' of monasticism, the Norsemen were uncouth, uneducated brutes, but they were able to hold the native

population down through lack of unified resistance. The Vikings were great traders, especially in slaves, and Dublin developed into a port and market-place.

The city savoured a brief spell without foreign rule when the Vikings, quarrelling among themselves, were driven out by a rare unity of Irish forces. By 917, however, they were back. This time, they concentrated on developing Dublin as a major fortified trading centre. They built Wood Quay on the south side of the Liffey and constructed permanent homes and other buildings in the surrounding area.

Old habits

They established towns in other parts of Ireland and developed commerce, but they could not change their ways completely. They continued their old habit of launching raids into the countryside, concentrating especially on the monasteries, where those distinctive round towers were built to act both as look-outs and secure shelters from the marauders.

The tables began to turn as the Irish started to get their act together, and Dublin repeatedly found itself under attack. In 980, Mael Sechnaill, King of Meath, was declared high-king of Ireland and was promptly challenged by the Viking commander, Olaf. Their forces met at Tara, north of Dublin, long a sacred place to the Irish. Olaf's army was thrashed. Sechnaill besieged Dublin four times in the next few years and the Vikings' grip began to weaken.

Towards the end of the 10th century a new dynasty emerged in the southwestern province of Munster under the kingship of Brian Boru, who gained a notable victory against the Norsemen in 999 and won recognition as high-king of Ireland in 1002. The Vikings supported a revolt against Boru from the province of Leinster, which included Dublin. They chose the wrong man and were defeated by Brian Boru once and for all at the Battle of Clontarf on Good Friday, 1014.

You can get an idea of what life was like in Viking Dublin at **Dublin's Viking Adventure** (*Essex Street West; tel: 679 6040; Tue–Sat 1000–1630; admission: ££; concessions*). This fanciful trip through time re-creates the sights, sounds and even smells of old 'Dyflin', as the Vikings knew it. The final section of the trip features an important collection of artefacts discovered in excavations at nearby Wood Quay and other parts of Viking Dublin.

Thingmote

The Thingmote, whose site is signposted from outside the Dublin Tourism Centre, was a 40ft-high earthen mound built by the Vikings around AD 1000. It stood on what is now the corner of Church Lane and Suffolk Street and was the location of the Norsemen's parliaments and assemblies. In medieval times the Thingmote was a place for public entertainment and executions. It was levelled in 1682 and the earth used to prevent flooding.

Christ Church Cathedral

The imposing bulk of Christ Church Cathedral stands on the site of a simple wooden structure built in 1038 by Sitric Silkenbeard, king of the Dublin Norsemen. Sitric also donated fertile farm lands which provided revenue for the cathedral until as recently as 1871.

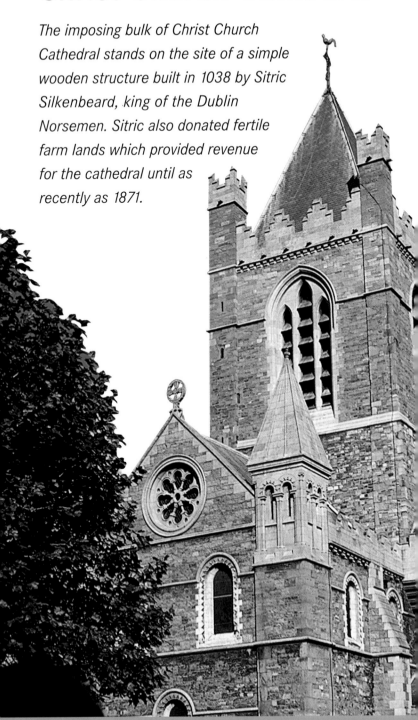

Work on the present structure began in 1172 under the Anglo-Normans, led by Richard de Clare, Earl of Pembroke, aka Strongbow, commander of the first invasion of Ireland from England. The planning committee for the project, which continued until 1220, consisted of Strongbow, his wife's uncle Archbishop Laurence O'Toole, and the Prior of Christ Church.

The first task was to dig out the huge crypt. Covering the entire area of the cathedral, the **crypt** survives as one of the largest in the British Isles.

For centuries, the British establishment in Ireland used the cathedral as their principal place of worship. Four Irish kings were knighted here in 1395 by Richard II, and Lambert Simnel (The Pretender) was crowned **Edward VI** of England in May 1487.

The cathedral went through a rough patch in the 16th century. In 1562 the roof collapsed, destroying the south arcade, most of the west front and Strongbow's tomb, later restored with the effigy of a knight whose identity has long been forgotten. The cloisters became a market-place and in the crypt 'tippling rooms' were established for drinking and smoking.

In 1821, **Skinners' Row**, later to be renamed Christchurch Place, was widened to show the cathedral to its best advantage. All it revealed, however, was that the building was on the verge of collapse. Henry Roe, a wealthy whiskey distiller, stepped in to underwrite the cost of reconstruction.

93

The heart of St Laurence O'Toole is preserved in a metal casket in St Laud's chapel at the east end of the cathedral. A glass case in the crypt contains the mummified bodies of a cat and a rat found in an organ pipe during restoration.

Christchurch Place. Tel: 677 8099.
Daily 1000–1700.

St Patrick's Cathedral

Nearly 20 years younger than Christ Church, St Patrick's stands on the oldest Christian site in Dublin. St Patrick is said to have baptised converts in a nearby well, and a church is known to have stood here since 450.

St Patrick arrived in the country in 432 from the British mainland, probably Wales. The son of a wealthy Christian, he was taken to Ireland as a slave at the age of 16 after being captured by pirates.

Patrick was bought by an Ulster chieftain and served as a shepherd, devoting himself to religion. After six years, he escaped and managed to get back to his home across the Irish Sea. He soon became driven by a desire to return to Ireland as a Christian evangelist, and to prepare himself he went to France, where he studied at Auxerre under St Germanus.

His religious superiors in France did not want him to return to Ireland as a missionary because they felt he lacked proper education, but Pope Celestine I overruled them when Palladius, the first Irish missionary bishop, died.

Mission accomplished

Never one for the easy path, Patrick went first to northern and western Ireland, where no Christian missionary had ever set foot. He became the trusted friend of tribal leaders and was soon making many converts. His mission was so successful – he is said to have baptised around 120,000 people and founded 300 churches – that he had to bring clergymen from Britain and France to help in the work.

Not everyone approved of Patrick, however. Many British churchmen were suspicious of him and opposed the way he ran his churches. But Patrick, serene and single-minded as ever, went his own way and preached in Ireland for the rest of his life.

The saint's name is linked with many an Irish legend. Everyone knows that it was he who drove all snakes out of the island, and that the shamrock became the symbol of Ireland after he used its three leaves to illustrate the Holy Trinity. But his greatest legacy, surely, is 17 March, St Patrick's Day, adopted as an annual fun day by people of all faiths in many parts of the world.

The present church

Poor relief

A private residence opposite the Olympia Theatre, in Dame Street, bears in large letters the name of the Sick and Indigent Roomkeepers' Society. Dublin's oldest charity, the society was founded in 1790 to provide relief for the city's poor and had its headquarters here from 1851 until a recent move to new premises.

In 1190 St Patrick's original church was rebuilt in stone by John Comyn, an Englishman who succeeded Laurence O'Toole as Archbishop of Dublin. It was elevated to the status of cathedral in 1213 and rebuilt in its present form between 1220 and 1250.

If Christ Church, barely 500m away, was regarded as the cathedral of the establishment, St Patrick's was much more the cathedral of the people. The fact that it was outside the city walls removed it from the influences and regulations of government.

St Patrick's inadvertently made an unusual contribution to the English language. The phrase 'chancing your arm', arose in 1492 when the Earl of Ormonde took refuge in the Chapter House during a feud with the Earl of Kildare. To settle the dispute, a hole was cut through the door so the two men could shake hands, without chancing more than an arm. You can still see the hole in the door.

St Patrick's Close. Tel: 475 4817. Apr–Oct Mon–Fri 0900–1600, Sat 0900–1700, Sun 1000–1100, 1215–1500; Nov–Mar Mon–Sat 0900–1600, Sun 1030–1100, 1245–1500.

Dublin Castle

Archaeologists have found evidence of a defensive rath or earthwork that existed on the site of Dublin Castle even before the Vikings arrived and built their fortress in 841. Strongbow, the Earl of Pembroke, also recognising its strategic position, had a motte on the site where the 13th-century Record Tower now stands.

King John ordered the castle to be built in 1204, and the first stage, consisting of a central circular keep and a curtain wall with massive towers, was completed around 1215. The keep survives as the Record Tower. It has also been known over the centuries as the Black Tower, the Gunner's Tower and the Wardrobe Tower. The only other survivor of the old castle is the Bermingham Tower, which was added in the 14th century.

Two large towers, with a drawbridge and portcullis, stood at the entrance in Castle Street, but were removed in the mid 18th century.

Colourful times

Like most structures of its kind and period, the castle has seen some colourful action. In 1534 it came under cannon-fire during the rebellion of Silken Thomas Fitzgerald. In the 1560s it was refurbished as a vice-regal residence and in 1591 the dashing rebel Red Hugh O'Donnell escaped from the Record Tower, then again the following year. The Irish Crown Jewels were stolen from the Bedford Tower in 1907, and have never been seen since. It was unsuccessfully attacked by insurgents in 1916.

Towards the end of the 17th century, the castle began to change both in function and structure, and total reconstruction began after 1684 when fire destroyed the vice-regal quarters. Reception rooms and offices were built, and in 1761 the Master of Ceremonies' apartments were completed. The Chapel Royal was built between 1807 and 1814.

> The actual course of Irish history from the late sixteenth century to the end of the eighteenth century provides abundant material for history lessons ... All you have to do is to leave out the atrocities committed by your side, and provide copious details of those committed by the enemy.
>
> **Conor Cruise O'Brien,**
> **Ancestral Voices, 1994**

From the mid 19th century the castle served as headquarters of the Dublin Metropolitan Police and housed the vice-regal offices and State apartments. It was handed over to the new Irish Government in 1922.

The castle's main gate, at the top end of Cork Hill, off Dame Street, is surmounted by Van Nost's *Statue of Justice* which, Dubliners observe, has its back turned on the city. The façade of the old Guard Room is preserved here and marks around the doorway show where British troops used to sharpen their bayonets.

Today, the castle is accessible to the public and there are guided tours. Built as the residential quarters of the vice-regal court, the magnificent State Apartments are now used for presidential inaugurations and state functions and also serve as the venue of Ireland's presidencies of the European Union. The State Apartments, Undercroft and Chapel Royal are normally open to visitors, but the State Apartments may be closed on occasions for State purposes.

The Chester Beatty Library and Gallery of Oriental Art, which was formerly housed at Ballsbridge, is due to reopen in Dublin Castle in due course. The priceless collection of Oriental art includes furniture, decorated manuscripts, paintings, ceramics and some of the earliest known biblical papyri. The collection is so large that curators estimate it will take 55 years to display everything in a rotating exhibition.

Old Dublin's streets and churches

The area where Dublin began is a great place for strolling. The labyrinthine streets encompass not only the city's two cathedrals and its ancient castle, but also a host of surprises.

City Hall

Topped by an impressive copper dome, City Hall, in Lord Edward Street was built in 1779. The present stone balustrade replaced an iron railing which collapsed under the weight of a crowd watching a public flogging in 1814; nine people died and many others were injured. In 1852 it was taken over by Dublin Corporation and since then has been the City Council's meeting place. Inside the entrance rotunda are statues of Daniel O'Connell and other historic figures. Frescoes adorn the walls. A superb view down Parliament Street, across the river and along Capel Street can be seen from the top of the steps. The Corporation has been in existence since 1192 and Lord Mayors have been elected annually since 1665.

Dublinia

St Michael's Hill, Christ Church. Tel: 679 4611. Apr–Sept daily 1000–1700; Oct–Mar Mon–Sat 1100–1600, Sun 1000–1630. Admission: ££; concessions.

Housed in the Synod Hall, which is linked to Christ Church Cathedral by a picturesque bridge, Dublinia is a multimedia presentation and re-creation of the medieval city. There is also an exhibition of Viking artefacts recovered from the Wood Quay archaeological site.

Marsh's Library

St Patrick's Close. Tel: 454 3511. Mon, Wed–Fri 1000–1245, 1400–1700; Sat 1030–1245. Admission: £.

Magnificently furnished with dark oak bookcases, Ireland's first public library has remained unchanged since it was built in 1701 by Archbishop Narcissus Marsh. Note the unusual three wire cages into which scholars were locked when consulting particularly valuable books. The library houses about 25,000 volumes, many of them exceptionally rare. It is still used by scholars and has a working bindery to conserve the books.

St Audoen's Church

Dublin's earliest surviving medieval church is St Audoen's, in High Street. It dates from 1190 and the tower houses three bells cast in 1423 and believed to be the oldest in Ireland. An early Christian gravestone in the porch has been kept at the church since before 1309 and is known as the 'Lucky Stone'. Behind the church, steps lead down to St Audoen's Arch, the only remaining gateway to the old city, which is flanked by sections of the 13th-century city walls.

Whitefriar Street Carmelite Church

The remains of St Valentine, the patron saint of lovers, are kept in Whitefriar Street Carmelite Church (*56 Aungier Street*). They were given to the church in 1835 by Pope Gregory XVI after they were exhumed from the cemetery of St Hippolytus in Rome, and now rest under a statue of the saint next to the high altar. The church also contains an oak statue of the Virgin and Child dating from the late 15th or early 16th century, and believed to be the only wooden religious figure to survive the Reformation in Ireland.

The Liberties

Francis Street and Thomas Street, west of the two cathedrals, mark the eastern and northern boundaries of a district known as The Liberties, a free-booting, devil-may-care area when it lay outside the old city walls, a tract of overcrowded, crime-ridden, festering slums by the end of the 18th century. Gentrification is encroaching on the narrow streets of small, red-brick houses, but there are still some parts where poverty is all too apparent.

Originally, there were four Liberties, which until the 16th century were under monastic jurisdiction, rather than the civic jurisdiction of the Mayor of Dublin. After Henry VIII's suppression of the monasteries, the Liberties were 'privatised' and granted to aristocratic favourites of the monarch.

The Liberties continued to enjoy a kind of free port independence – St Patrick's Liberty, the smallest with an area of only 9 acres, for example, was able to offer sanctuary to defaulting debtors into the 19th century.

An Act of Parliament of 1841 changed the city's administration and opened the door over the next 20 years for the abolition of the Liberties. Until recently, however, the change seemed to have been little more than a legality: the Liberties continued to be different and apart from the rest of Dublin, and to some extent they continue to be so to this day.

The Liberties is now noted for its antiques and craft items. Francis Street is the focal point for collectors and dealers. Here, you'll find shops selling old advertising boards and enamel signs, garden statuary, vintage fireplaces, pine furniture, lamps, medals and coins, and there are craftsmen to repair, clean or restore them.

Iveagh Market, at the northern end of Francis Street, opened in 1907 and is housed in an intriguing Victorian building, with arches adorned by the carved heads of Moors and oriental traders. One carving, of a grinning and winking Occidental, is said to be that of Lord Iveagh, who established the market and was head of the Guinness brewing family at the time.

The Tivoli (*135–138 Francis Street; tel: 454 4472*) started out as a cinema in 1936, closed in the 1970s and reopened as a theatre in 1987. Today it is one of the city's most modern and technologically sophisticated theatres, staging a variety of live entertainment – from drama and musicals to Irish and international shows.

The Church of SS Augustine and John, better known to Dubliners as **St John's Lane Church**, on Thomas Street, is an elaborate building, designed by Edward Welby Pugin and built between 1862 and 1895. James Pearse, father of the Pearse brothers who were executed in 1916, sculpted the apostles in the niches of the spire. It stands on the site of the ancient Abbey of St John which in medieval times provided a hospital for incurables.

> *I went out that night in the cold smells of Dublin and last streaks of light. Down Dame Street with hope and massive heart.*

J P Donleavy, *The Ginger Man*

Eating and drinking

You won't have far to look for food or drink in Old Dublin. There seem to be restaurants and pubs on every corner – and in between, too. At lunchtime, especially, you can't help wondering who's keeping the city's wheels turning while all these people are enjoying themselves.

Auriga

6 Temple Bar. Tel: 671 8228. ££. The décor is a bit Zen-like, but there's an eclectic menu and a reasonable wine list. *Daily 1730–2230.*

Il Baccaro

Meeting House Square, off Eustace Street. Tel: 671 4597. £–££. Piquant, garlicky snacks and wine in a little bit of old Italy. Hard to eavesdrop, since most conversations are in Italian, but good for people-watching. *Daily 1800–2300.*

Botticelli

3 Temple Bar. Tel: 672 7289. ££. Another Italian institution, but this time they serve whole meals rather than snacks. Some Dubliners say this is the best place for pasta and pizzas. Reservations essential. *Lunch and dinner daily.*

Burdock's

2 Werburgh Street. Tel: 454 0306. £. Now this really is an institution – the city's oldest fish and chip shop. Strictly take-away fresh fish with chips made from Irish potatoes. No place for vegetarians, though – the exquisite chips are fried in beef dripping. *Mon–Fri 1230–midnight, Sat 1400–2300, Sun 1600–midnight.*

Eden

Sycamore Street, off Dame Street. Tel: 670 5372. ££. Fashionable and chic, but justifiably popular because the standard of food is excellent – international and Irish dishes prepared with flair. *Lunch and dinner Mon–Sat.*

Les Frères Jacques

74 Dame Street. Tel: 679 4555. £££. As you might expect, the cuisine here is classic French. The restaurant is next door to the Olympia Theatre, and a pianist plays at weekends. *Lunch Mon–Fri, dinner Mon–Sat.*

Lord Edward

23 Christchurch Place. Tel: 454 2420. ££–£££. The city's oldest seafood restaurant (*circa* 1968) offers dishes that reflect its experience. Lunch is served in the ground floor pub, dinner in the upstairs restaurant. *Lunch Mon–Fri, dinner Mon–Sat.*

Mermaid Café

60–70 Dame Street. Tel: 670 8236.
£–££. Very imaginative cuisine from
Ben Gorman, one of Ireland's leading
chefs. Reasonably priced and served in
light and airy surroundings. *Lunch*
and dinner Mon–Sat, brunch and
dinner (to 2130) Sun.

Old Dublin

90–1 Francis Street. Tel: 454 2028.
££–£££. The spirit of Viking Dublin
lingers on in the menu, an eccentric
mix of Scandinavian and Irish dishes;
Russian, too, if you feel like a change.
Lunch Mon–Fri, dinner Mon–Sat.

Pubs

The Brazen Head

20 Bridge Street Lower. Tel: 677 9549.
Dublin's oldest pub was built in the
1660s, but it stands on the site of an
inn that first opened in 1198 – so it
claims to be more than 800 years old.
Lots of atmosphere, with stone walls,
open fires, traditional music and sing-
along sessions.

Mother Redcap's Tavern

Back Lane, off Cornmarket. Tel: 453
8306. With its stone walls and oak
beams it looks like a genuine 17th-
century tavern, but it actually dates
from 1988. The atmosphere is lively
enough and it's handy for Mother
Redcap's Market next door.

Porterhouse Brewing Company

Parliament Street. Tel: 679 8847.
Real ale enthusiasts will be in their
element here in Dublin's only micro-
brewery pub.

Stag's Head

1 Dame Court. Tel: 679 3701. They
started drinking here in 1770, but the
place was rebuilt in 1896 so the décor
is authentic Victorian, right down to the
oak and mahogany bar, brass lamps,
antique mirrors and cosy snugs.

Jonathan Swift

The world can be grateful that Jonathan Swift (1667–1745) failed to achieve his political ambitions. He was disappointed, to say the least, at being given a senior church position in Ireland instead of England. But had he not been appointed Dean of St Patrick's Cathedral, he would probably have been no more than a spin doctor for the Tory party of the day rather than one of the greatest satirists in literary history.

Swift's bitter-sweet satire, savage yet humorous, underlined his concerns about the way people treated each other in his time – especially the behaviour of the English towards the Irish – yet his writings remain fresh and are relevant to many of today's social conditions.

Born of English parents in Dublin, Swift graduated from Trinity College and in 1688 or 1689 moved to England where he became secretary to the statesman Sir William Temple, an appointment he held, off and on, until 1699. In 1695 he became a minister in the Church of Ireland.

While working for Temple, Swift met Esther Johnson – he called her Stella – who became his lifelong companion. Swift wrote many long letters to her, which were published after his death as the *Journal to Stella*. Swift and Stella now lie side by side in St Patrick's Cathedral.

Return to Ireland

Soon after Temple's death in 1699, Swift became the pastor of a small parish in Ireland. He made many visits to England between 1701 and 1710, gaining influential friends in government circles and making a name for himself as a skilful writer. He became a powerful supporter of the Tory government and wrote many articles defending Tory policies. As a background spokesman for the government, he was in effect an early spin doctor.

In recognition of his political work, Queen Anne appointed him **Dean of St Patrick's Cathedral**, a disappointment for him because he really wanted a church position in England. A year later, in 1714, the Queen died and George I took the throne. Swift's political hopes were dashed later that year when the Whigs came into power.

Disheartened, he spent the rest of his life at St Patrick's and, although he yearned for England, he switched his political energies to supporting the cause of the Irish against British abuses. He wrote *Gulliver's Travels*, *The Drapier's Letter*, *A Modest Proposal* and many satirical pamphlets. In his last years, Swift's physical and mental health declined and he died on 19 October 1745.

> **" Here He Lies, Where Savage Indignation Can No Longer Lacerate His Heart! "**

Swift's epitaph, written by himself, over his tomb in St Patrick's Cathedral

Swift left his money to found St Patrick's Hospital for the mentally ill. Modernised and considerably enlarged, the hospital still exists near Heuston Station.

A bust of the Dean stands close to his grave in the west end of the nave. His pulpit, chair and other belongings are displayed in the north transept with a collection of his works.

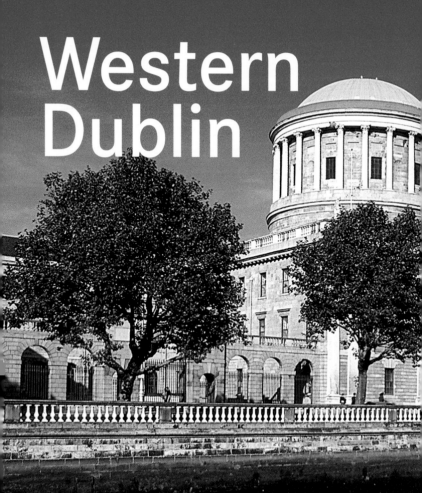

Western Dublin

*Dublin's northwestern section includes the Old
Jameson Distillery, St Michan's Church and the
great cobblestoned expanse of Smithfield, laid out
in the 1630s as a market-place and open space
for the people in a fast-growing city. Smithfield is
poised for cultural development in 1999. The River
Liffey becomes more recreational as it flows by
Phoenix Park. South of the river are such major
attractions as Kilmainham Gaol, the Irish Museum
of Modern Art and the Guinness Hop Store.*

WESTERN DUBLIN

Getting there: Heuston Station, on the DART line, is the best start point for exploring Western Dublin.

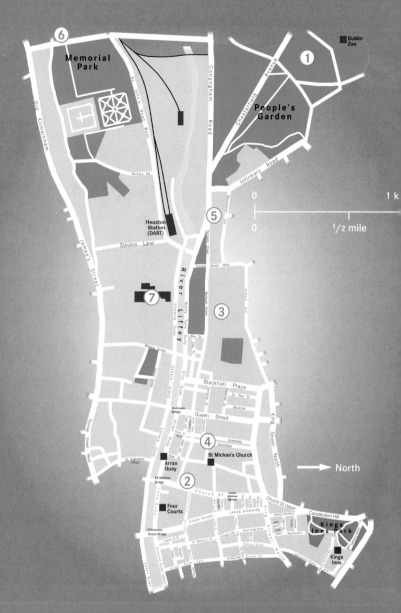

WESTERN DUBLIN

① Phoenix Park

Even in a compact capital like Dublin, it's good to relax in the wide open spaces of Europe's biggest enclosed park. Many species of mature trees and the chance of seeing deer make this a pleasant place in which to stroll at any time of year. **Pages 114–115**

② Cheers!

Take a tour to the Old Jameson Distillery in Bow Street and you'll thoroughly appreciate the 1400 years of industry and tradition behind your glass of Irish whiskey. At the end of the tour you can take the taste test. **Page 112**

③ Old barracks, new museum

Nearly three centuries of military history make Collins Barracks the ideal new venue for thousands of exhibits for which the overflowing National Museum of Ireland's Kildare Street property was formerly the only showcase. **Page 113**

④ Yea or neigh?

Normally, ancient Smithfield is a quiet area, but every now and again, early on a Sunday morning, it echoes with the ring of steel horseshoes on the cobblestones as a horse fair takes place. **Pages 112–113**

⑤ Ryan's

Anyone with an interest in the Victorian age should call in at Ryan's (Bongo Ryan's to the locals, for some mysterious reason), near Phoenix Park's main entrance. This big pub is as Victorian as they come: brass gas lamps, antique mirrors, carved mahogany bar, a couple of snugs. There's great service and good bar snacks at lunchtime and in the evening, and if it's the chef's day off you can still get soup and sandwiches. **Page 121**

⑥ Kilmainham Gaol

Ireland's troubled history is documented in this 18th-century gaol transformed into a thought-provoking museum. **Pages 116–117**

⑦ Guinness Hop Store

Sample 'the black stuff', learn how it is made and enjoy the wit of the famous Guinness advertising campaigns. **Page 119**

King's Inns

The building is not open to the public.

This imposing building, standing in King's Inn Park, was the last work by the English architect James Gandon. Constitution Hill provides a good view of the inns, topped by a central dome. Although the foundation stone was laid in 1795, there were all sorts of hitches and delays and it was many years before the building, a place in which barristers could study, was completed. You can see the exterior and walk under the central archway and (except on Sundays when it is closed) through a gate into Henrietta Street.

Four Courts

Inns Quay. Tel: 872 5555.

The great dome of Gandon's inspired edifice beside the Liffey can be seen from many parts of Dublin, lording it over Inns Quay without any pretence of modesty. But it was among the first casualties of the Civil War in 1922, when anti-Treaty forces occupied the building, and held siege for two months. Enormous damage was done when government troops fired shots at them for three days, then a terrible blaze added to the destruction. Restoration work took ten years. Figures above the portico represent Moses, Justice (*shown left*) and Mercy. The four original courts were Common Pleas, Chancery, Exchequer and King's Bench. Now the building houses the High Court, Supreme Court and district courts.

Fruit and Vegetable Market

For more than a century Dublin Corporation Fruit and Vegetable Market has been housed in an ornate Victorian building in St Mary's Lane. It is entered through a wide archway bearing the city arms. Tall, narrow windows are set in the red and yellow brickwork.

St Michan's Church

Church Street, Dublin. Tel: 872 4154. Mid Mar–Oct Mon–Fri 1000–1645; Nov–mid Mar Mon–Fri 1000–1245; Sat 1000–1245 all year. Admission: £.

St Michan's Church (Church of Ireland) dates from 1685, and stands on the site of an 11th-century church built by the Danes. Handel is believed to have played the organ (still in use) while composing his *Messiah*. The church is noted for the exquisite carvings of violins and other instruments from a single block of wood. Amazingly well-preserved mummified bodies lying in the crypt are the big draw. Although the wooden coffins, probably 200 years old, split open, the bodies were preserved by the effect of moisture-absorbing limestone. Tours are available.

" *Dublin is so much more than purely spectacular. She is impregnated with a past that never evaporates ... Every quarter ... has, in fact, got a character you could cut with a knife.* "
Novelist Elizabeth Bowen, 1930

Smithfield Village

The wide cobbled area which is Smithfield has been a market-square since the 17th century. Surrounded by warehouses and other old buildings, it is being developed as Smithfield Village Complex, a cultural and retail centre which includes the Old Jameson Distillery (see below). Horse and cattle sales took place here, and horse fairs are still held occasionally in summer.

Old Jameson Distillery

Bow Street. Tel: 807 2355. Daily 0930–1800 (last tour 1700).
Admission: ££; concessions.

An audio-visual presentation traces the 1400-year history of Irish whiskey-making. The fascinating tour ends with a tasting session.

Blue-Coat School

Walk westward from Arran Quay and neighbouring Ellis Quay and turn right into Blackhall Place to see the Blue-Coat School, built to Thomas Ivory's design. Work on the building, in which poor children were housed and educated and where disabled Dubliners could lodge, began in 1669. It was founded by a royal charter. The traditional blue uniform was worn until the 1920s. The school has moved out of Dublin and the building is now the headquarters of the Incorporated Law Society of Ireland.

Collins Barracks

Benburg Street. Tel: 677 7444. Tue–Sat 1000–1700, Sun 1400–1700. Free.

Set on an 18-acre site, this dates from 1701 and claims the distinction of being Europe's oldest military barracks and the world's oldest continuously-occupied barracks – almost 300 years.

FLORA

In 1994 the property was acquired by the National Museum of Ireland. It now houses weaponry, decorative arts and countless other fine exhibits on two floors. Visitors can see a 2000-year-old Japanese ceremonial bell, gauntlets worn by King William at the Battle of the Boyne (1690) and Wolfe Tone's pocket book, which he kept with him during his incarceration at the barracks in 1798 – the year of the Rebellion.

In 1985 a monument was erected at the barracks where men who were executed for their part in the Rebellion are buried. Formerly known as the Royal Barracks, the imposing building of Wicklow granite was renamed after Michael Collins, the revolutionary who was killed in the Civil War in 1922.

❝ *It is a city of ghosts, but ghosts of the so nearly dead that something of their earthly presence still lingers in the wide streets, the pleasant squares, that were their homes.* ❞

Honor Tracy, journalist and author, from *Mind You, I've Said Nothing*, 1953

Phoenix Park

Right on Dublin's northwestern doorstep, less than 2 miles from the city centre, lies the enormous Phoenix Park, providing nearly 1800 acres of recreational land, enclosed by 7 miles of wall. It claims to be the largest enclosed city park in Europe and is five times as big as London's Hyde Park. More than one million people attended when Pope John Paul II celebrated Mass in Phoenix Park in 1979. A 90ft steel cross commemorates the event.

The park's origins go back to 1662 when land was acquired for a royal deer park. It wasn't until the mid 18th century that it was recognised as a public recreation area. Around this time Lord Chesterfield erected the Phoenix Column, but a taller obelisk, built in 1817 to mark the Duke of Wellington's defeat of Napoleon and standing 200ft high, catches the attention of passers-by in the roads surrounding the park.

Several gates lead into the park. The main entrance, Park Gate, leads from Conyngham Road, which runs parallel with the River Liffey. The main artery through the park is Chesterfield Avenue, and a road leads round the perimeter. Near Park Gate is the People's Garden, set out beside a lake in the 1860s. The official residences of the President

of Ireland and the American ambassador are in Phoenix Park. Many Dubliners go jogging in the park; others take their exercise on the cycle trails and running tracks. Playing fields cater for a range of spectator sports, including Gaelic football and hurling, while grassy open spaces where deer are sometimes seen, and wooded areas, make the park a pleasant place to stroll at any time of year.

A Visitor Centre in 17th-century Ashtown Castle shows an audio-visual presentation of activities and happenings in the park through the ages.

Dublin Zoo

Summer Mon–Sat 0930–1800, Sun 1030–1800; in winter to sunset.
Admission: £££; concessions.

Thirty acres of Phoenix Park are home to animals from many parts of the world. Dublin Zoo, established around 1831, is thought to be the third oldest in the world. It is known for its rare and endangered animals and for its breeding programmes. One of its major successes is the breeding of lions in captivity, and the famous MGM lion was born in Dublin Zoo.

An educational discovery centre, a daily 'Meet the Keeper' opportunity, feeding programmes, a children's corner with pigs, sheep, goats and fluffy guinea pigs, train rides and a children's play area are popular features.

Gibbons, chimpanzees, orang-utans and spider monkeys cavort on Monkey Islands in the lakes. The World of Cats presents African and Asian species, and polar bears and other animals and birds in the Arctic section are a big draw.

Murder in the park

One May morning in 1882, Lord Cavendish, the newly appointed Chief Secretary for Ireland, and Thomas Burke, his Under Secretary, were walking in Phoenix Park close to the Vice-Regal Lodge – now the official home of the President of Ireland. They were set upon and knifed to death. The assassinations, in which surgical knives were used, were the work of a group of the Invincibles, a breakaway section of the Fenian movement. The suspects were taken to Kilmainham Gaol. Five of them were executed and others were imprisoned.

Kilmainham Gaol

A grim island set amongst quiet suburban streets, Kilmainham Gaol is a disquieting museum. It tells two stories: outlining penal reform towards the end of the 18th century and plotting the course of Ireland's struggle for independence from British rule.

When it opened in 1796 on a site disconcertingly known as Gallows Hill, Kilmainham Gaol was considered a model prison. Up to that time, criminals and debtors – men, women and children – were simply locked up and more or less left

to their own devices. If they had money they had a reasonably easy time; if not, they suffered the ravages of sickness and malnutrition. There was no thought in those days of rehabilitation.

Kilmainham opened with 52 individual cells. Prison reformers at that time believed fresh air solved many problems, so prisoners suffered from cold and damp as well as the psychological effects of almost solitary confinement. Soon, over-crowding became a burden, too.

After the 1798 Rebellion political prisoners joined the ordinary inmates, and in 1803, when Robert Emmet's insurrection failed, some 200 rebels were jailed. Emmet himself was executed. The prison was enlarged, which merely provided the authorities with more room for the incarceration of independence activists. Many died at the hands of the public executioner; luckier ones were transported to Australia.

The last prisoner

Tip

Newspaper tycoon Alfred Harmsworth – later Lord Northcliffe – was born in 1865 in the Liffey-side village of Chapelizod, near Phoenix Park, Dublin.

Charles Stewart Parnell spent six months in Kilmainham in 1881–2, but he lived in relative comfort, taking over the Governor's quarters for most of his sentence. The last political leader to be kept in the prison – indeed, he was the last prisoner of all – was Eamon de Valera, later to serve as Ireland's prime minister and president.

Kilmainham closed with the release of de Valera on 16 July 1924. The old gaol was allowed to fall into decay and by 1960 was a roofless ruin when a group of veterans from the 1916 era decided it should be restored as a national monument. It took a force of volunteers more than 20 years to complete the restoration. Today, Kilmainham's cells are empty of prisoners, but full of poignancy.

An exhibition area near the prison entrance depicts a number of the events that took place within Kilmainham and there are memorabilia associated with former inmates, as well as a video presentation. In the main courtyard is the *Asgard*,

the yacht owned by Erskine Childers, author of *Riddle of the Sands* and a Republican who was executed during the Civil War in 1922. Childers and his wife Molly used the *Asgard* to smuggle rifles from Germany for the Irish Volunteers in July 1914. Many of the guns were used in the 1916 Rising.

117

Inchicore Road, Dublin 8. Tel: 453 5984. Apr–Sept daily 0930–1800 (last tour 1630); Oct–Mar Mon–Fri 0930–1700 (last tour 1600), Sun 1000–1800 (last tour 1630). Admission: ££; concessions.

Around Southwest Dublin

At first glance, southwest Dublin might seem a rather melancholy area. In addition to Kilmainham Gaol, it also has three historic hospitals – one still in use as such and another, said to be the finest 18th-century building in Ireland, now housing the country's major gallery of modern art. In a lighter mood, perhaps, there is the Guinness Brewery.

Dr Steevens' Hospital (*Steevens' Lane, Dublin 8*), was named after Richard Steevens (1653–1710) who studied theology at Trinity College before taking a degree in medicine in 1687. A wealthy man, he bequeathed his estate to his twin sister, Grizel, with the proviso that on her death the residue was to be used to build a hospital. Grizel decided not to wait. Retaining £100 a year for herself, she ordered the building of the hospital, which opened in 1733. She lived there until her death at the age of 93 in 1747. The hospital closed in 1987.

> " *Recently I walked through the slums, clearances, tumbledowns of Pimlico, from which I could see, at every turn, the Dublin Mountains.* "
>
> **Austin Clarke, from *Twice Round the Black Church*, 1963**

Also in Steevens' Lane is **St Patrick's Hospital**, founded in 1745 as the result of a bequest by Dean Swift (*see pages 104–105*). Still in use, it is the oldest psychiatric hospital in Ireland and is pre-dated in the British Isles only by the Bethlem Hospital in London. Originally the hospital held up to 54 patients, but the building was doubled in size in 1778. By 1815 it housed nearly 200 patients. A charter was granted in 1888 enabling fees to be charged on a non-profit basis because Swift's original bequest could no longer finance the hospital.

Irish Museum of Modern Art

Military Road, Dublin 8. Tel: 612 9900. Tue–Sat 1000–1730, Sun 1200–1730. Free.

The former Royal Hospital Kilmainham is now home to the **Irish Museum of Modern Art**. Through its permanent collection and temporary exhibitions, the museum presents an

exciting range of contemporary Irish and international art. Drama and musical performances are also staged, and there are continuing community and educational programmes.

The Royal Hospital opened in 1684 to accommodate 300 maimed and infirm soldiers. It was designed by the Irish Surveyor-General, Sir William Robinson, and was styled on Les Invalides in Paris, with a formal façade and an elegant courtyard. At first people were so impressed by the building's beauty that it was suggested it should be used instead to house Trinity College, but it remained a hospital for almost 250 years. The building was restored by the Irish government in 1986 and needed only minimum alterations to accommodate the museum. There is a coffee shop, book shop and banqueting and catering facilities.

Guinness Hop Store

James's Gate, Crane Street, Dublin 8. Tel: 453 6700, ext 5155. Oct–Mar Mon–Sat 0930–1600, Sun and public holidays 1200–1600; Apr–Sept Mon–Sat 0930–1700, Sun and public holidays 1030–1630. Admission: ££; concessions.

The south bank of the River Liffey in this part of the city is dominated by the mass of the Guinness Brewery, home of the famous creamy black stout which is now produced worldwide at the rate of more than 10 million glasses a day.

A 19th-century, four-storey building of the old brewery complex has been converted into the **Guinness Hop Store**. There is a fascinating audio-visual exhibition on the history of Guinness in Ireland, as well as a cooperage and transport museum, a souvenir shop and a convivial bar where you can relax and sample the 'Black Stuff'. A recent addition is a display of Guinness's famous advertising.

Shopping

The Winding Stair

40 Lower Ormond Quay. A labyrinthine second-hand bookshop on four floors, overlooking the Liffey. The café serves good fresh soup and bread.

Francis Street (*see page 101*)

is one of the city's most famous 'antiques highways'. Here, and in surrounding streets such as the Coombe, there are plenty of shops for treasure hunting. You might rub shoulders with celebrities at **O'Sullivan Antiques** (*43–44 Francis Street*), where the speciality is 18th- and 19th-century furniture. Another good spot for antiques, where you may find a bargain, is Ormond Quay and Bachelors Walk, along the Liffey.

Mother Redcap's Market

High Street. Open Friday to Sunday, 1000 to 1700. An indoor market full of antiques and bric-à-brac. Next door is the Iveagh Market (*see page 101*), a good place for bargains in second-hand clothes.

Pubs

O'Shea's Merchant

*12 Lower Bridge Street. Tel: 679 3797.
£.* Good craic at this lively pub, with
ballad sessions every night and set
dancing. Traditional and modern Irish
food is also served.

Out on the Liffey

27 Ormond Quay. Gay and lesbian pub
on the riverside.

Ryan's

*28 Parkgate Street. Tel: 671 9352
££–£££. Restaurant open Mon–Fri
1230–1430 and Tue–Sat 1930–2230.
Closed Sun and Mon dinner.* This
splendid Victorian pub, with its dark
mahogany bar and private snugs, is
an old Dublin gem, just before the
entrance to Phoenix Park. Its small,
intimate dining room serves modern
Irish cuisine, game and Mediterranean
dishes and is highly recommended.

Slattery's

129 Capel Street. Tel: 872 7971. £.
A lively pub with a mix of traditional
music, rock and blues, and set dancing.
It also serves a good carvery lunch
and evening snacks.

Zanzibar

35–36 Ormond Quay. Decadently
decked out in a Persian theme with
enormous Turkish urns, this steamy
watering hole is hugely popular with
the locals.

Restaurants

Hole in the Wall

*Blackhorse Avenue. Tel: 838 9491
£–££.* Located at the edge of Phoenix
Park, the Hole in the Wall claims to be
the longest public house in Europe. It
is equally famous for its traditional
Irish music and Sunday lunchtime
carvery. The restaurant serves good
food all week long.

Nancy Hands

*30–32 Parkgate Street. Tel: (1800)
400 018. £–££.* A brilliant new pub
and restaurant beside the Collins
Barracks National Museum serving
steaks and Irish cuisine, both modern
and traditional dishes.

Boss Crokers Bar
& Restaurant

39 Arran Quay. Tel: 872 2400 ££.
Northern Italian and Cajun fare in a
pub-style restaurant.

Liadain's Restaurant

17 Ranelagh. Tel: 497 8240. £££. A
warm and welcoming gourmet Irish
restaurant serving traditional cuisine,
accompanied by music.

The Easter Rising

The Easter Rising of 1916, which still looms large in the Irish collective memory, was born out of a complex set of issues – social, political, emotional, and intellectual.

For generations, the people of Ireland had seen their religion and their language reviled; they had suffered appalling injustices and famine. Politically, with the abolition of the Irish Parliament and the assumption of direct rule from Westminster, they had been downgraded.

By the end of the 19th century people began to feel they had had enough. There was a stirring of national aspirations and national pride. There was also a stirring of defiance – popular, angry defiance – against the British who occupied their land, and an intellectual stirring – a mushrooming of cultural nationalism that expressed itself principally in literature. In 1893 the Gaelic League was founded to revive the Irish language, and this was followed by the growth of a literary movement led by the poet, W B Yeats.

Soon the intellectuals moved to the barricades: three Irish language poets – Patrick Pearse, Joseph Plunkett and Thomas MacDonagh – were among those who signed the 1916 Proclamation of the Irish Republic.

Dublin's response

Thoughts of wrenching independence from Britain by force began to harden in 1912 when the Westminster government again failed to implement a Home Rule Bill. When the armed Ulster Volunteer Force was formed to resist Home Rule,

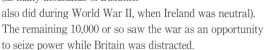

Dublin responded with the founding of the Irish Volunteer Force to support the Home Rule movement.

The outbreak of World War I split the Volunteer movement. About 200,000 of them went to fight with the British Army (as many thousands of Irishmen also did during World War II, when Ireland was neutral). The remaining 10,000 or so saw the war as an opportunity to seize power while Britain was distracted.

On the morning of 24 April 1916 – Easter Monday – Patrick Pearse mounted the steps of the General Post Office building on O'Connell Street and read the Proclamation of a Republic (*see page 27*). Fighting soon broke out, and although they held out at strategic positions around the city, the rebels were soon overwhelmed by the British. They surrendered after five days.

The British wasted no time in dealing with the insurgents, and because there was a state of war they were able to deal with them under martial law. The 14 rebel leaders were court-martialled, charged with treason and sentenced to death. Within three weeks of Pearse's reading of the Proclamation, all 14 were dead – executed by firing squad in the sombre stone-breakers' yard at Kilmainham Gaol (*see pages 116–117*).

Just a few hours before his death, Joseph Plunkett, one of the rebels, married the young artist Grace Gifford in the prison's Roman Catholic chapel, where tours of the gaol now begin. After the ceremony, the young bride waited outside Kilmainham's gates until a volley of shots from beyond the wall told her she was a widow.

123

Outer Dublin

Close to Dublin are dozens of places of interest and leisure activities – beaches, fishing villages, country towns, castles, factory shops, golf courses, water skiing, equestrian centres, mountain walks, horse racing, monastic remains, bird sanctuaries, boat trips, stately homes, botanic gardens. The DART (Dublin Area Rapid Transport) has more than two dozen stations along Dublin Bay giving easy access.

OUTER DUBLIN

Best of Outer Dublin

Getting there: many of the sights in this chapter can be reached by DART railway, but some are best visited by car.

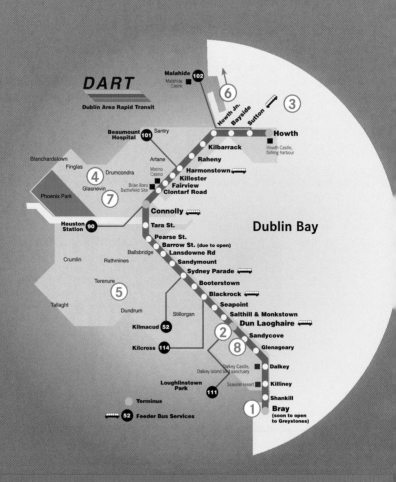

DART
Dublin Area Rapid Transit

Malahide **102**
Malahide Castle

6

3

Howth Jn. Bayside Sutton

Beaumount Hospital **101** Santry

Howth
Howth Castle, fishing harbour

Kilbarrack

Blanchardstown Finglas

4 Drumcondra

Artane

Raheny

Harmonstown

Killester

Glasnevin

Brian Boru Battlefield Site

Fairview

Phoenix Park

7

Marino Casino

Clontarf Road

Connolly

Dublin Bay

Heuston Station **90**

Tara St.

Pearse St.

Barrow St. (due to open)

Lansdowne Rd

Crumlin

Rathmines

Ballsbridge

Sandymount

Terenure

Sydney Parade

Booterstown

5

Blackrock

Tallaght

Dundrum

Stillorgan

Seapoint

Salthill & Monkstown

Kilmacud **52**

Dun Laoghaire

2

Sandycove

Kilcross **114**

8

Glenageary

Dalkey Castle, Dalkey Island bird sanctuary

Dalkey

Loughlinstown Park **111**

Seaside resort

Killiney

Shankill

Terminus

1

Bray
(soon to open to Greystones)

52 Feeder Bus Services

① Stately shopping

However many stately homes and gardens you've seen, Powerscourt House and Gardens is one not to miss. Apart from the obvious attractions and walks, it has speciality shops and a garden centre. **Page 128**

② Help!

Sample a powerboat-style pounding with the Dublin Bay Sea Thrill from Dun Laoghaire. They provide all the gear, you provide the nerve. It's 40 minutes of sheer excitement, with or without a barbecue to follow.
Page 131

③ Ireland's Eye

The small craggy island called Ireland's Eye is a fascinating bird sanctuary. Boatmen run trips there in summer.
Page 135

④ R.I.P.

Many of Ireland's revolutionaries and political figures are buried in Glasnevin Cemetery, and their gravestones make interesting reading. Even better are the stories behind them, which you can hear on the twice-weekly guided tour – and it's free. **Pages 138–139**

⑤ School museum

Patrick Pearse, a signatory to the Proclamation at Dublin GPO – the Easter Rising of 1916 – founded a bilingual school at Rathfarnham in 1910. It is now a museum, with an audio-visual show about Pearse and the school, a nature study room and exhibitions. **Pages 142–143**

⑥ Seaside fun

For safe bathing, sandy beaches, a possible glimpse of seals, video games and a good selection of pubs and restaurants, go to Skerries.
Pages 140–141

⑦ Plants galore

Twenty thousand plant species, from alpines to a weeping cedar, grow in the extensive grounds and glasshouses of the National Botanic Gardens in Glasnevin. **Page 139**

⑧ Ulysses remembered

In the early 1900s James Joyce spent a week as a guest in the Martello tower at Sandycove. Later he set the first chapter of *Ulysses* in it. Now it contains a museum dedicated to the writer, his life, work and characters. **Page 130**

Bray, Killiney and Dalkey

Bray

At the southern limit of the DART, 14 miles from Dublin, Bray has more than a mile of sand and shingle beach. On warm summer days crowds flock along the esplanade and into the amusement arcades. This was one of Ireland's earliest resorts when sea bathing became popular in the Victorian era. Bray Head, nearly 800ft high, provides bracing cliff walks.

The National Aquarium (*The Esplanade; tel: 286 4688; admission: £*) presents a fascinating array of marine life. Its policy of conservation through education indicates what can be done to help endangered species. Thousands of fish and other creatures are exhibited.

Bray has a much-acclaimed Greek-Cypriot restaurant, the Tree of Idleness (*tel: 286 3498; ££*). Just up the coast at Shankill is a Cooper's restaurant (*tel: 284 2037; £–££*) – one of several around Dublin, each individually owned and operated, where you can rely on good-value fish, steak and game.

About 2 miles southwest of Bray is Powerscourt House and Gardens estate (*Enniskerry; tel: 286 7676; daily 0930–1730; admission: ££*). The interior of the Palladian-style house, built in the 1730s, was severely damaged by fire in 1974. Restoration includes a galleried ballroom and craft and speciality shops. A garden centre, terrace café, children's playground, picnic area, 45 acres of formal and walled gardens, terraces, statuary, lakes and walks provide a good day out.

Four miles away, accessible on foot from the gardens, is a magnificent

River Dargle waterfall, with a drop of more than 300ft. *Daily 1030–1900, in winter to dusk. Admission: £.*

Killiney

The DART station at Killiney (3.5 miles north of Bray) is right on the pebbly beach, which stretches for 2 miles. People come from miles around to swim here. The coast road in this area has stupendous views, and it's worth sprinting (or panting) up the hill in Killiney Park for the view of the bay.

Dalkey

Dalkey ($1^1/4$ miles north of Killiney) is a small medieval town with much to charm and interest the visitor. It once had seven castles or tower houses; two still remain. One, dating from the 15th century, houses a well-presented heritage centre, and you can enjoy the views from the battlements. An audio-visual show illustrates Dalkey's development from the Middle Ages, while exhibits introduce many aspects of the town, its two harbours and two piers and some of its former residents, including J M Synge, George Bernard Shaw and James Joyce.

Today the Dalkey area still attracts the famous – Maeve Binchy, Damon Hill, Chris de Burgh, Bono and members of U2 are said to have homes there. St Begnet's 7th-century church is near the heritage centre.

In summer a boat ferries passengers from Coliemore Harbour to Dalkey Island, 15 minutes away. This is a bird sanctuary, where wild goats can be seen defying gravity on the rocky crags. A Martello tower still stands on the island.

129

Eating at P D's Woodhouse Barbecue Bistro (*1 Coliemore Road, Dalkey; tel: 284 9399; £–££*) is fun and the food, cooked on an open oak-burning grill, is excellent.

Authentic Thai cuisine cooked to perfection has earned the Thai House (*Railway Road; tel: 284 7304; £££*) a high reputation.

Queens (*Castle Street; tel: 285 4569; ££*) is an award-winning pub with a well-recommended restaurant.

Sandycove and Dun Laoghaire

Sandycove

In the week he spent in the Martello tower at Sandycove in 1904 as a guest of the tenant, Oliver St John Gogarty, James Joyce amassed enough material to use in the opening chapter of his most famous book, *Ulysses*. Since 1962 the tower has housed a delightful little **museum** displaying Joyce first editions, photographs, letters and personal possessions, including his guitar, waistcoat, cigar case and the trunk he used when travelling. Items associated with Joyce's Dublin, portraits of the writer and his death mask are also exhibited. *Tel: 280 9265. Apr–Oct Mon–Sat 1000–1700, Sun and public holidays 1400–1800. £. Combined tickets for the James Joyce Museum and the Writers Museum in Dublin are available.*

Dun Laoghaire

If you arrived in Ireland by sea from England or Wales you will already have seen something of Dun Laoghaire (pronounced Dun Leary). It's a busy seaport for freight as well as passengers, and its waterfront is its best aspect. Work on the present harbour began in 1817. Two piers, each $1^1/2$ miles long, were also constructed, one with a bandstand.

You may strike lucky and be serenaded by music on a summer's day and sometimes a **puppet theatre** performs. Dun Laoghaire's prosperity is reflected in the number of sailing boats bobbing at anchor in summer. Water skiing and other sports are catered for, and daredevils will relish the exhilaration of the **Dublin Bay Sea Thrill's** bucking broncho tactics.

Housed in the former 1830s Mariners' Church, the **National Maritime Museum** unfolds some interesting stories (*Haigh Terrace; tel: 280 0968; May–Sept Tue–Sun 1430–1730; admission: £*). One of these concerns the ship that laid the first transatlantic telegraph cable more than 130 years ago. A French longboat on display was captured in Bantry Bay, Co Cork, in December 1796, when Wolfe Tone's attempted invasion was thwarted by stormy weather.

With fish straight from harbour to plate, via the kitchen, the **Brasserie na Mara** (*1 Harbour Road; tel: 280 6767; ££–£££*), successfully keeps up its reputation. The restaurant, overlooking the harbour and adjacent to the DART station, is in what used to be a Victorian railway terminal. Highly popular – best to book.

Good wine, inspired cuisine and modest prices bring back Dubliners time and time again to **Morel's Bistro** (*18 Glasthule Road; tel: 230 0210; ££*).

Dun Laoghaire also offers Indian and Cajun cuisine. **Krishna** (*upstairs at 17 Georges Street Lower; tel: 280 1855; ££*) serves Northern Indian dishes. Evening opening is gratifyingly late – to 2330 Sun–Thur and 0030 Fri and Sat.

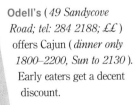

Odell's (*49 Sandycove Road; tel: 284 2188; ££*) offers Cajun (*dinner only 1800–2200, Sun to 2130*). Early eaters get a decent discount.

Monkstown to Booterstown

Monkstown

Monkstown, a fashionable Dublin suburb half a mile from Dun Laoghaire, is distinguished by its unusual Church of Ireland church designed by John Semple, partly in Moorish style, with a central tower, four corner towers and turrets. The remains of **Monkstown Castle**, south of the town, can be seen. It was founded by Cistercian monks – hence the name.

The **Irish Cultural Institute** in Belgrave Square is the headquarters of one of Ireland's foremost traditional music societies. Music and dance performances are held there in summer.

> Dublin on the east, the Europe-regarding coast of Ireland, owes her vitality and complexity as a city to a continuous influx of foreign life.
>
> **Elizabeth Bowen**

Racing tip

Dublin's horseracing enthusiasts migrate 6 miles south of the city to Leopardstown when National Hunt or flat racing events take place.

Blackrock

With two of its finest 18th-century houses demolished in the 1970s and 1980s to make way for flats and a supermarket, Blackrock (1 mile north of Monkstown) can no longer be regarded as a village. A dormitory for Dublin, it still offers good sea views and bathing. People come here for its two good shopping centres and speciality shops. More than 50 stalls sell antiques, crafts and bric-à-brac at the weekend market. Handcut crystal can be bought at **Dublin Crystal's** factory shop (*Brookfield Terrace; tel: 288 7932*). You can have your purchases engraved.

Ayumi-Ya, in Blackrock's Newport Centre, has been a popular Japanese dining spot since the 1980s. The Japanese chef cooks some dishes at the table (*evenings only; ££*).

A mainly marshy area at Rock Road, **Booterstown**, is an important bird sanctuary.

Then there were the rude bold children who had no shoes and the cripples who swung along on crutches with a jaunty kind of insolence through the slum streets.

Louis MacNeice, The Strings Are False, 1965

133

Sandymount and Howth

Sandymount

Sandymount Strand (2 miles southeast of central Dublin) is a smooth, sandy and – especially when the tide is out – spacious beach, handy for people from central Dublin. The tide goes out more than a mile, and rushes back in so fast that it is dangerous for swimmers.

Lansdowne Road is a name to make the heart beat faster if you're a rugby fan. Excitement runs high when international matches are played, and the cheering when it's a home win reverberates around the local streets. If you're not a fan, avoid Lansdowne Road DART station at the close of a match. If you are, then you'll find like-minded souls at **Kitty O'Shea's Bar** (*Upper Grand Canal Street; £*). There's a good lunchtime buffet and evening bar food.

Howth

Situated out on a promontory at the northeastern end of Dublin Bay, Howth is an attractive village at the northern end of the DART line, and is the northernmost point of Dublin Bay. It offers a range of watersports and has a marina for pleasure craft. This busy commercial fishing port is generally a good strolling area for visitors and there's always something going on – fishermen cleaning their sturdy boats or a group of youngsters getting soaked during instruction on surfboard control. The harbour piers also provide good walks.

Howth was the main harbour on this coastline before Dun Laoghaire was developed. It was at Howth in 1914 that Erskine Childers, author of *Riddle of the Sands*, landed German guns and ammunition from his yacht *Asgard*, for the Irish Volunteers. Photographs of people unloading the arms are displayed in the National Museum of Ireland (*see page 61*). The *Asgard* herself is currently exhibited in the main courtyard at Kilmainham Gaol (*see pages 116–117*), but may be moved at some time to the National Museum's Collins Barracks premises.

Howth Head rises dramatically 170m from the sea. Go along Balscaddan Road at the eastern end of Howth for the cliff walk towards the **Baily Lighthouse** (about 1¹/2 miles). The sea views along the peninsula are wonderful.

The 16th-century **Abbey Tavern** (*tel: 839 0307; ££*), with flagstone floors and turf fire, which overlooks the harbour, serves delicious seafood – fish, crab, lobster and the famous Dublin Bay prawns.

Also of high repute is the **King Sitric Fish Restaurant** on the East Pier (*tel: 832 5235; £££*), where perfectly cooked fresh fish is served with organic vegetables.

Inspired menus and a gift for unlikely pairings of foods – like dropping some whiskey into fish chowder – and getting it right makes **Adrian's** (*Abbey Street; tel: 839 1696; ££*) an exciting place to eat.

The grounds of 17th-century **Howth Castle**, behind the Deer Park Hotel, are worth seeing, particularly in late spring when countless varieties of rhododendron are in bloom (*open daily 0800 to sunset*). The castle itself is closed to the public. Also in the grounds is a neolithic dolmen, the remains of the square tower of 16th-century Corr Castle and the **National Transport Museum** (*open Easter–Sept daily, 1000–1800; weekends only rest of year*). The exhibits here include horse-drawn commercial vehicles, carriages, fire-fighting appliances, early motor vehicles and the Hill of Howth tram. This superb open-top tram served Howth until 40 years ago.

A little island called **Ireland's Eye**, a mile offshore, is a bird sanctuary where puffins and other sea birds can be seen at close quarters. Boat trips go there in summer, and a daily service is operated by Frank Doyle (*tel: 087 678211*). The island, which has a Martello tower and an old church, was the site of a monastery nearly 1500 years ago.

Malahide

Beyond the strand and dunes of Portmarnock, the seaside town of Malahide (7$^1/_2$ miles northeast of central Dublin), with its narrow streets and cosy pubs and restaurants, has a new marina development flanked by smart apartments and shops.

The enormous structure of Malahide Castle is the big attraction here. The castle has stood for more than eight centuries. One family, the Talbots, lived in it for most of that time, from 1185 until 1973, when the last Lord Talbot died. Their only brief period of absence was when Oliver Cromwell sent them packing.

Many additions and alterations have been made through the centuries. As visitors pause by beautiful period furniture and portraits of the family and various historic figures, fascinating aspects of the castle and its residents unfold. As well as English, tours are available in German, Spanish, Italian, French, Dutch and Japanese.

The long table in the Great Hall is the same one at which 14 members of the Talbot family breakfasted together before setting out for the Battle of the Boyne in 1690. Every one of them was killed that day.

Botanic Gardens and Model Railway

The castle's 250-acre grounds include the Talbot Botanic Gardens and the Fry Model Railway Museum. The Talbot Botanic Gardens contain 5000 labelled species representing Ireland's largest collection of southern hemisphere plants.

Children enjoy the Fry Model Railway Museum, but no one can fail to be charmed by this admirable presentation of miniaturised trains, railway stations, bridges, trams, buses, the Liffey, river craft and recognisable Dublin landmarks. The Irish and foreign locomotives and trains are superbly crafted models from the early days of the railways to more

recent times. The collection began over 70 years ago, when a railway engineer and draughtsman, Cyril Fry, meticulously produced each model in detail. When you have taken in every detail, call in at the model shop and bookshop.

Castle. Tel: 846 2184. Apr–Oct Mon–Sat 1000–1700, Sun and public holidays 1400–1700; Nov–Mar Mon–Fri 1000–1700, Sat, Sun and public holidays 1400–1700. Admission: £; concessions; family ticket available. Talbot Botanic Gardens. Tel: 846 2456. May–Sept daily 1400–1700. Fry Model Railway Museum. Apr–Sept Mon–Fri 1000–1800, Sat 1000–1700, Sun and public holidays 1400–1700. Admission; £; concessions; family ticket available. Combined Castle/Fry Model Railway/Newbridge House ticket available.

One of the features of **Smyth's of Malahide** (*12 New Street; tel: 845 3128*) is its American-style Fun Food Menu. Texas ribs and chargrilled steaks are specialities. *Lunch £, dinner ££.*

Charters (*5 St James Terrace; tel: 845 0833; £££*), offers classic French cuisine. *Open evenings, closed Sun and Mon.*

For Italian tastes, try seafood or meat dishes at **Bon Appetit** (*9 St James Terrace; tel: 845 0314; lunch ££, dinner £££*) or **Giovanni's** (*Townsend; tel: 845 1733*), which serves Italian and vegetarians food and steaks (*lunch £, dinner ££*).

North of Dublin

*The region from just west of the city in the Liffey Valley and northeastwards to the coast is a golfer's heaven, with more than two dozen courses. One of the closest to the city, and welcoming to all, is half a mile north of the airport. The **Open Golf Centre's** pay-and-play parkland course (27 holes) has a floodlit under-cover driving range, full-time professional teaching staff, golf shop and clubs and equipment for hire (*Newtown House, St Margaret's, Co Dublin; tel: 864 0324; daily*).*

There are also half a dozen riding centres and a wealth of ancient monuments, some of which you will just happen across as you drive around. One of the earliest ecclesiastical settlements surviving in Ireland today, which includes a 9th-century round tower and an effigy tomb, is at Lusk. **Lusk Heritage Centre** occupies a 16th-century belfry (*tel: 843 7683; Fri mid June–mid Sept*) and has an exhibition relating to medieval churches in County Dublin.

Glasnevin

About 2 miles north of Dublin, on the N2 road, is Glasnevin, whose cemetery is famous as the last resting place of the people who shaped Ireland – Prime Minister Eamon de Valera, Charles Stewart Parnell, Daniel O'Connell, Michael Collins and others, many of whom were executed. A free guided tour unravels the details of who did what for their country, and why. *Tel: 830 133. Tours leave from the main entrance at 1430 Wed and Fri.*

Cast-iron glasshouses, a palm house, a lily house and 50 acres of gardens with at least 20,000 plant species are open to the public at the **National Botanic Gardens**. The gardens, on the south bank of the River Tolka, were founded by the Royal Dublin Society in 1795. A rose garden, rock garden, arboretum, new alpine house, weeping Atlantic cedar, large pond and area of tropical water plants and succulents provide plenty for the avid gardener to enjoy. The glasshouses, built between 1843 and 1869, and the 1884 palm house, containing tropical plants, orchids and ferns, have recently been restored.

National Botanic Gardens: Tel: 837 7596. Summer Mon–Sat 0900–1800, Sun 1100–1800; winter Mon–Sat 1000–1630, Sun 1100–1630 (restricted hours for glasshouses). Free.

Donabate

Visitors will find plenty to interest them at **Newbridge House**, 12 miles north of the city at Donabate. The manor's interior is considered to be a fine example of Georgian domestic living, with much stucco plasterwork by Robert West. Original furniture is in place in reception rooms which can be toured, the kitchen has authentic utensils of the period and there's an 18th-century laundry. Built in 1737 for the Archbishop of Dublin, Newbridge House is set in 350 acres of parkland. The courtyard has been fully restored with a blacksmith's forge, carpenter's shop, dairy and estate worker's home, all with tools and artefacts. A craft shop and coffee shop are on site. In the park is a 25-acre traditional farm, with sheep, poultry and farmyard animals.

Newbridge House: Tel: 843 6534. Apr–Sept Tue–Fri 1000–1700, Sat 1100–1800, Sun and public holidays 1400–1800 (closed Mon); Oct–Mar Sat, Sun and public holidays 1400–1700. Admission: £; concessions; family ticket available.

Skerries area

Skerries (18 miles northeast of Dublin) is Fingal County's prize coastal resort. It has safe bathing, sandy beaches, a pretty harbour with fishing boats and pleasure craft.

Playful seals often add to the idyllic scene. Shops sell local arts and crafts, a free playground keeps the children happy, golf and tennis facilities are handy, and walkers can follow a route round the headland. **Bob's**, at South Strand, is a family entertainment centre with pool, slots, videos and children's rides.

With crowds of holidaymakers to feed in summer, Skerries has a good selection of places to eat and drink.

Owner-chef Terry McCoy's **Red Bank Restaurant** in Church Street won the Egon Ronay Seafood Restaurant of the Year award in 1995 and the master's touch remains. Fish and shellfish are beautifully cooked and presented. *Tel: 849 1005. Open Tue–Sat 1900–2200. £££.*

The family-run **Waterfront** in Harbour Road, serves fresh fish, vegetarian meals, steaks and general meat dishes. Gluten-free dishes and children's meals are available. Home-grown produce is used. In suitable weather you can dine *al fresco. Tel: 849 1964. Tue–Fri 1100–1500, 1730–2200, Sat 1100–2200, Sun 1100–2030. ££.*

Moriarty's Windmill, 17 New Street, claims to have the most comprehensive menu in the Dublin area. There's live music at weekends. *Tel: 849 1215. Daily 1230–1500 and Mon–Sat from 1800, Sun from 1700. Bar food served daily 1230–1800. Restaurant ££–£££, bar food £.*

Ardgillan Demesne

Tel: 849 2212. Apr–Sept Tue–Sun and public holidays 1100–1800, Oct–Mar Wed–Sun and public holidays 1100–1630. Closed 20 Dec–end Jan, except Sun 1400–1600. Park daily 1000–dusk. Admission: Castle £.

On the elevated coastline north of Skerries, off the N1, on the way to Balbriggan, one of the few industrial areas of northern Co Dublin, is Ardgillan Demesne. From here there are splendid views along the coast. Set in nearly 200 acres of pasture and dense woodland, Ardgillan overlooks the Bay of Drogheda. The grounds are a haven for many bird and animal species. In the castle is a permanent exhibition of maps from a 17th-century survey of Ireland. Ground floor rooms with Georgian and Victorian furnishings and ornaments and the basement kitchen are open to the public. The rose garden, walled kitchen garden and a Victorian conservatory are a pleasure to visit, and there are picnic areas and tearooms on the site.

Marino Casino

Tel: 833 1618. June–Sept daily 0930–1830; May and Oct daily 1000–1700, Nov and Feb–Apr Sun and Wed noon–1600. Admission: £.

If you are travelling to or from the northeast of Dublin look for the Marino Casino at Fairview Park, not a gambling centre but a summer house built in the 1760s for Lord Charlemont. It is hailed by some as one of the finest classical buildings of its period in Europe, though to the layman its exterior may seem squat and ostentatiously ornamented. It is guarded by four stone lions. The chimneys are out of sight, encased in rooftop urns, and drains are concealed in stately columns. The interior is undeniably impressive; 16 beautifully decorated rooms on three floors have antique furniture, silk hangings and grand fireplaces, and the State Room is even more richly ornate.

Around Rathfarnham

The Dublin Mountains are gentle and picturesque. Pick clear weather to walk, or, more accurately, climb, up the rocky path at Three Rock Mountain. From the top you can take in panoramic views over Dublin and Wicklow.

Try to spend some time in the **Rathfarnham** area, where there is a castle, three parks and a museum that will set you thinking.

Rathfarnham Castle (3 miles south of Dublin) was the home of the Jesuits for many years, and has recently undergone much restoration. It is thought to

date from 1583, and was declared a national monument four centuries later. Interior renovations were carried out in the 18th century. *June–Sept daily 1000–1800, May and Oct daily 1000–1700. Tel: 661 3111 for variable winter opening times. Admission: £.*

Bushy Park, Rathfarnham, is a peaceful place for a stroll or a picnic.

Not far away is **Marlay Park**, popular with families. It has a golf course, miniature railway, craft studios, lakes, woods and parkland, and marks one end of the long-distance Wicklow Way walk.

The **Pearse Museum**, in the lovely grounds of St Enda's Park, is housed in the former school which patriot and poet Patrick Pearse ran from 1910 until he was executed, aged 37, for his leading part in the 1916 Easter Rising. The school was a progressive, bilingual establishment for boys. Patrick's brother, Willy – also executed after the Rising – helped run it. The museum sheds light on the nationalist feeling and sense of injustice and outrage experienced by many Irish men and women, who were prepared to give their lives for their cause. An audio-visual presentation and a nature study room displaying Irish flora and fauna give an extra dimension to the museum. *St Enda's Park, Grange Road. Tel: 493 4208. Daily all year. Times vary. Free.*

Angling, canoeing, boating, golf and a riverside walk can be enjoyed in the Liffey Valley in South Dublin. A tributary of the Liffey, the Griffeen River, is crossed by the ancient **King John's Bridge** at Lucan, where a 120-acre park provides pleasant walks.

Another place for riverside walking is the linear park of the Dodder Valley. The Dodder can be followed from the Dublin Mountains through South Dublin.

If this makes you hungry and thirsty, you could call in at **Ashton's** at Clonskeagh, Dublin 6. It's a large pub on several levels, renowned for its walnut and hazelnut bread, home-made soups, hot roasts, cold buffet and salad bar. Outdoor seating provides a view of the River Dodder and its waterfowl. *Tel: 283 0045. Bar food 1230–1430, 1800–2130. £–££.*

Loreto Abbey

Near Rathfarnham is Loreto Abbey, home of the Loreto order of nuns. A young Albanian novice spent a year there in 1928 to learn English, then left to work in Calcutta. She became Mother Teresa.

PROFILE

The difference an 'e' makes

Only an 'e' marks the difference in spelling, but purists will tell you that the two products are as different as chalk and cheese. We're talking alcohol, of course. Whiskey in Ireland – without the 'e' in Scotland. Both are made from barley and are the result of distillation. Beyond that point, Scottish and Irish distillers part company.

The characteristic smoky flavour of Scotch comes from the open peat fires over which the malted barley is dried. The Irish, surprisingly, considering how much peat they have

and burn, dry their barley in smoke-free, coke-fired kilns. The result is a clear, clean barley taste.

The Irish also point out that their whiskey is distilled three times, while most similar spirits produced in Scotland and elsewhere are distilled only twice. They also claim their product came first.

Distillation was first practised in the Middle East, long before the birth of Christ. The process was mentioned by Aristotle in the 4th century BC, but in the beginning it was used solely for making perfume.

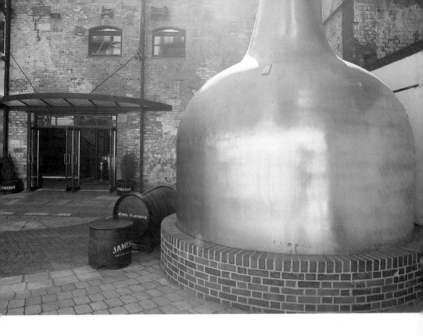

The Irish put the art to better use when distillation was introduced to them by Christian missionaries around AD 600. They made a product for internal consumption only and named it Uisce Beatha (pronounced *Ishkay Ba-ha*), meaning 'the water of life'. The phrase was too difficult for English soldiers serving in Ireland in the 12th century – even after drinking the stuff – so they shortened the name to whiskey.

At one time the Irish landscape was dotted with distilleries – more than 2000 were known to be in operation – but today there are only two (to say nothing of a few moonshiners making *potheen* in quiet country corners). Between them, the distilleries at Midleton, Co Cork, and Bushmills, Co Antrim, make the full range of individual whiskeys which are as distinctive in taste as the labels on their bottles.

Despite their reputation, the Irish, it seems, are not a nation of drinkers. Official statistics claim that 50 per cent of the population is teetotal. 'But the other half more than make up for them,' says a Dublin tour guide.

EXCURSIONS

Excursions

The Historic North

Less than an hour's drive to the north of Dublin, surrounding the town of Navan in County Meath, lie some of Ireland's most sacred and historic sites.

Boyne Valley Archaeological Site

Boyne Valley Archaeological Site. Tel: 041 24488. June–mid Sept, daily 1000–1900; mid Mar–May and mid Sept–Oct daily 1000–1300, 1400–1700; Nov–mid Mar Tue–Sun 1000–1300, 1400–1630. Admission: £.

The Boyne Valley Archaeological Site, flanking the N51 between Navan and Drogheda to the east, embraces more than 40 monuments. These range from earthworks and standing stones to the massive megalithic structures at Newgrange.

Newgrange is one of the most important Stone Age sites in Europe. More than 4000 years old and pre-dating the Egyptian pyramids, the Newgrange passage grave is awe-inspiring. The mound covering the tomb is constructed of water-rolled pebbles and rises to a height of 35ft and is surrounded by an incomplete circle of stones. Massive stones line the passage and strange geometrical symbols and spirals are inscribed on the rock.

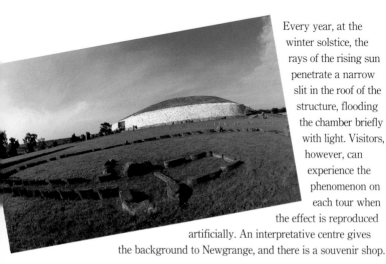

Every year, at the winter solstice, the rays of the rising sun penetrate a narrow slit in the roof of the structure, flooding the chamber briefly with light. Visitors, however, can experience the phenomenon on each tour when the effect is reproduced artificially. An interpretative centre gives the background to Newgrange, and there is a souvenir shop.

Slane Hill

According to tradition, Slane Hill, about 7 miles northeast of Navan, is where St Patrick first preached the Christian message to the Irish in 433. From the top there is a superb view of the Boyne Valley, the site on 1 July 1690 of the Battle of the Boyne which saw the defeat of the Catholic James II of England by William of Orange.

Kells

Kells – *Ceanannus Mór* in Irish, which is how you will see it on the signposts – is where the famous illuminated manuscript, now at Trinity College Dublin, is believed to have been produced. A copy of the *Book of Kells* is displayed in St Columba's Church of Ireland, where the gallery also has other exhibits relating to Kells and the monastery founded by St Columba.

The monastery was built in the 6th century, and in the 9th century served as a sanctuary for monks from Iona, in Scotland, who had fled from Viking raiders. The site encloses a 100ft-high round tower from the 11th century, several 9th-century high crosses and the 7th-century St Columba's House, a small stone oratory with a steeply pitched roof. Kells is 10 miles northwest of Navan.

Hill of Tara

The Hill of Tara, 8 miles south of Navan, near the village of Kilmessan, was the seat of the high kings and the political and spiritual centre of Celtic Ireland. A passage tomb was built some 4000 years ago and although the site continued to be important in early Christian times it was abandoned in 1022. The site itself, which consists of grassy mounds, wide ditches and earthworks, is freely accessible daily year-round, but there is a charge for entering the nearby interpretative centre, where guided tours begin. *Tel: 046 25903.*

The Road to Bally K

Avoca, in County Wicklow, south of Dublin, attracts thousands of visitors who know it as the location of Ballykissangel in the eponymous television series.

By car, Avoca can be reached from Dublin comfortably within 90 minutes, travelling along the N11 to Arklow or Wicklow, but a more rewarding route, in terms of scenery, is to follow the old **Military Road**, the R115, from Dundrum, south of Dublin, and across the Wicklow Mountains.

The Military Road was built across the mountains by British troops who were out to quash Irish rebels after the 1798 Rebellion. The countryside is wild, the views stupendous, the weather fickle and it is not difficult to imagine the hardships suffered by those who built the road.

Glenmacnass, south of the remote pass known as Sally Gap, brings you unexpectedly back into contact with other humans and their cars lined along the roadside. The attraction: a waterfall tumbling dramatically over rocks as a river is squeezed into a deep, narrow glen.

The village of **Laragh**, at the southern end of the Military Road, is not much more than a handful of buildings at a crossroads, but it offers the welcome bonus of a pub, **Lynhams**, where good, reasonably priced food, is served in surroundings reminiscent of an alpine lodge.

A mile or so from Laragh is **Glendalough**, the lakeside site of a monastic settlement founded by St Kevin in the 6th century. Stunningly located, it is County Wicklow's principal historic attraction, and among its extensive ruins are a near-perfect round tower, a 10th-century cathedral, an early church with Romanesque decoration and an oratory known as St Kevin's Kitchen. There is also an interpretative centre. *Tel: 0404 45351. June–mid Sept daily 1000–1900, closing times vary at other times of year. Closed Mon Nov–mid Mar. Admission charge.*

Avoca itself is a pretty village set at the heart of a gentle valley. Almost everyone calls in at **Avoca Handweavers** (*tel: 0402 35105; Mon–Fri 0930–1730, Sat–Sun 1000–1730*), the oldest mill of its kind in Ireland, still producing tweeds and other textiles by traditional methods. The showroom has a bargain section selling end-of-line garments for men and women, and there is a pleasant café.

If you return to Dublin by the coast road, you can visit **Mount Usher Gardens**. Laid out along the banks of the River Vartry in 1868, these 'wild' gardens contain rare trees, shrubs and flowers from all over the world. *Ashford, off N11 north of Wicklow. Tel: 0404 40205. Mid Mar–Oct Mon–Sat 1030–1800, Sun 1100–1800. Admission: £.*

Kildare

Anyone who loves horses and racing should be sure to make the 32-mile drive along the N7 to Kildare town, the heart of the Irish horse racing world.

Kildare's people live and breathe racing and most of its visitors are not tourists but race-goers. The Curragh, Ireland's famous flat-racing venue, is 4 miles to the east.

The Irish have an innate affinity with horses which knows no class or money barriers, yet it was a Scotsman, William Hall-Walker, later Lord Wavertree, who was the inspiration behind the **Irish National Stud** at Tully, just south of Kildare.

He was a man of ideas, some of which other people found baffling. His work at Tully began in 1900. Firmly believing that the destiny of horses (and all other creatures) lay in the stars, he built the stables with skylights to enhance the astrological influences. His breeding of thoroughbred horses was highly successful; they thrived on the rich grass and the mineral water from a lake fed by the River Tully.

Today the Irish bloodstock industry is among the most respected in the world. With nearly 300 horse boxes, its own saddlery and forge, the National Stud occupies around 1000 acres. Stallions with gleaming coats and rippling muscles, graze in paddocks alongside the Oak Walk. The Tully Walk passes by paddocks where mares and foals live when the breeding season is over.

A museum outlines the history of the horse and its importance in Ireland. Here equestrian items are displayed and the prize exhibit is the skeleton of the racehorse Arkle, the 1960s phenomenon.

A new visitor centre has a craft shop, restaurant and children's Lego area.

Sharing the same estate as the Irish National Stud are the **Japanese Gardens**. Devised by Hall-Walker, they were laid out by a Japanese, Tassa Eida, and his son, Minoru, between 1906 and 1910. The gardens symbolically depict the soul's journey through life, passing through the Hill of Learning, the Hill of Ambition, the Well of Wisdom, the Red Bridge of Life and other landmarks to the Garden of Peace and Contentment. Asian flowers, shrubs and trees, including bonsai, a miniature Japanese village and a tea house are seen along the way.

Irish National Stud and Japanese Gardens, Tully, Kildare. Tel: 045 521617. Mid Feb–mid Nov daily 0930–1800. Admission: £.

St Brigid's Cathedral (Church of Ireland) in Kildare town dates from the 13th century, with much restoration in Victorian times (*Market Square; daily 1000–1800; donations welcome*). It is on the site where St Brigid founded a community of monks and nuns in the 5th century. In the graveyard is a **Round Tower**, believed to be from the 12th century. At 108ft it is one of the highest in Ireland. *May–Sept daily 1000–1800, rest of year Sun only 1400–1700. Admission: £.*

153

“ *Half the world seemed to smell of horses, old harness, hay, oats, bran mashes, old stables and hub grease ... Now of course there is the strong, insistent, determined smell of petrol.* „

Jack Yeats, artist brother of poet and dramatist W B Yeats, writing in 1930

Kilkenny

Just over 70 miles southeast of Dublin – less than 2 hours by car – is Kilkenny, recognised as the finest example of a medieval settlement in Ireland. What is today the county seat originated from this monastic site.

Kilkenny, on the River Nore, is a rewarding town to see on foot. You should take time to stand and relish the sight of the medieval buildings and bright shop fronts.

A visit to the **Shee Alms House** is worthwhile. This hospital for the poor for three centuries, founded by Sir Richard Shee in 1588, is now the home of the Tourist Information Centre. You will also find the CityScope exhibition here. This is a miniature, three-dimensional scale model of Kilkenny as it was in the 17th century, with other small-scale exhibits, providing a different perspective on what you see outside. *Rose Inn Street. Tel: 056 21755. May–Sept Mon–Sat 0900–1800, Sun 1000–1630, Oct–Apr Tue–Sun 0900–1715; note: closed 1245–1400 Sun. Admission: £.*

Kilkenny is known as the Marble City – the locally quarried black stone is much in evidence in **St Canice's Cathedral**, which was completed in 1285. It has a commanding hilltop position, and though this is one of the buildings that Cromwell knocked about a bit, it is one of Ireland's finest cathedrals, rich in timber carvings and stained glass. Some of the tombstone effigies depict descendants of the Normans.

The Round Tower in the cathedral grounds provides a rewarding view from the top for anyone prepared to climb nearly 170 steps. *Dean Street. Tel: 056 21516. Mon–Sat 0900–1800 (closed 1300–1400), Sun 1400–1800. Donations welcome.*

The black capes of Dominican friars led to the name of the **Black Abbey**, founded in 1225. *Abbey Street. Tel: 056 21279. Daily.*

Kilkenny Castle is one of the nation's grandest and was occupied by the Butler family from the 14th century to the 1930s. It rises massively beside the River Nore in nearly 50 acres of parkland. Built in the 12th century, and with much Victorian alteration, it is especially known for its 150ft Long Gallery, which has a hammer beam and glass roof. *The Parade. Tel: 056 21450. Daily June–Sept 1000–1900; Oct–Mar Tue–Sat 1030–1700, Sun 1100–1700; Apr and May daily 1030–1700. Admission: £ for castle, grounds free.*

Kilkenny is known for its high-quality crafts – handwoven textiles, knitwear, heraldic jewellery and distinctive pottery are found in its shops. Take a look at the **Kilkenny Design Centre** in the old stableyard of the castle.

155

Always popular with tourists, Kilkenny is packed in late August when the town's annual Arts Week takes place. Art exhibitions, musical performances – classical, folk and jazz – and literary readings are among the events.

The Midlands

The delightful and historic countryside of Ireland's Midlands region, with its many castles and monasteries, is within easy reach of Dublin. Tullamore, the seat of Co Offaly, is only 64 miles from Dublin and is more or less halfway between the capital city and Galway on the west coast. From Tullamore to the fascinating Georgian town of Birr, also in Co Offaly, is another 23 miles.

The route from Dublin to Tullamore could be called the Canal Course. If you choose to follow the N4 to Kinnegad, then the N6 towards Tullamore, you follow the Royal Canal for much of the way. Or you could leave the N4 at Enfield, take the R402 and follow the Grand Canal into Tullamore.

Tullamore

Offaly's county seat is very much a canal town, and it's easy to imagine it in its heyday, with passenger and freight boats passing to and fro between Dublin and the River Shannon. The town is best known as the home of Tullamore Dew whiskey and the liqueur called Irish Mist. If you fancy a boating holiday, **Celtic Canal Cruisers** (*24th Lock; tel: 0506 21861*) have narrow boats for hire.

A mile outside Tullamore, on the N52 to Birr, is **Charleville Castle**. In a region bristling with ancient castles in varying states of ruin, this one is a bit of cheat. It is castellated and in the Gothic style – but it dates from only 1812. Nevertheless, it is a magnificent building, designed by Francis Johnston, the architect responsible for many of Dublin's splendid Georgian buildings. There are guided tours. *Tel: 0506 21279. May weekends only 1400–1700; June–Sept Wed–Sun 1100–1700. Admission: £.*

Birr

Birr is a gem, a virtually intact Georgian town with houses and mansions along tree-lined malls and avenues. The town lies at the heart of what was once the kingdom of Ely O'Carroll, the country of the O'Carroll dynasty who ruled for about 400 years from the early 14th century.

The main attraction today is **Birr Castle Demesne**. The castle, built in the early 18th century, is the seat of the earls of Rosse and is not open to the public, but the surrounding 100 acres of grounds are, and really should not be missed. There are formal gardens based on a 17th-century layout which include the world's tallest box hedges, recorded in the *Guinness Book of Records* at a height of 32ft as well as more than 1000 species of trees and shrubs, many very rare, from all parts of the world.

Laid out around a lake and along the banks of two rivers, the grounds also contain the restored 72in reflecting telescope which was built in 1845 and remained the world's largest for 75 years. It is now back in perfect working order after being dismantled in 1914. *Tel: 0509 20336. Apr–Oct daily 0900–1800, Nov–Mar daily 0900–1300, 1400–dusk. Admission: £; concessions.*

By the Shannon

Everyone who visits Ireland should set aside enough time to see the Shannon, that majestic river that flows through the heart of the country, flanked by ancient woodlands, offering sanctuary to an abundance of birdlife and flora and studded with some of the island's finest historical sites.

Athlone

Athlone straddles the Shannon in Co Westmeath and lies 77 miles west of Dublin, a comfortable two-hour drive along the N4 and N6. It's a busy town, a major road and rail junction on the border of the ancient provinces of Leinster and Connacht whose importance sprang from its position as a crossing point on the river.

The town's major attraction – apart from its shops – is 13th-century **Athlone Castle** (*Market Square; tel: 0902 72107; Apr–Sept daily 1000–1800; admission: £*). The castle offers a good introduction to the region, with exhibitions and audio-visual presentations on the flora, fauna and power resources of the Shannon, the 1691 Siege of Athlone which followed the Battle of the Boyne, and folk and military history. A special presentation features the life and career of the celebrated tenor, Count John McCormack, who was born in the town. The castle also houses a tourist office, art exhibitions and a tea room.

Boat trips along the river to nearby Lough Ree and Clonmacnoise (*see opposite*) leave from the quay opposite the castle.

Clonmacnoise

Clonmacnoise, near Shannonbridge, 12 miles south of Athlone, is one of Ireland's most impressive early Christian monastic sites (*tel: 0905 74195; daily 1000–1800; June–Sept 0900– 1900; admission: £*). The settlement was founded by St

Ciaran in 545. Standing at the crossroads of ancient Ireland's major north–south and east–west routes, it became one of the country's most sacred places, a centre of scholarship and piety and a burial place for the kings of Connacht and Tara. Today, the settlement presents a magnificent sight on a wide sweep of the Shannon. There are two round towers, the remains of a cathedral, ruined churches, high crosses and more than 200 decorated grave slabs. The excellent visitors' centre, housed in three buildings modelled on the beehive-shaped huts used by early monks, contains exhibition areas and a museum with early grave slabs and three original high crosses.

A surprisingly entertaining and informative trip across the extensive Blackwater Peat Bog is offered by the **Clonmacnoise and West Offaly Railway** (*Blackwater Works, Shannonbridge; tel: 0905 74114; Apr–Oct daily, tours on the hour 1000–1700; admission: £*). Organised by the Bord Na Móna (the Irish Peat Board), the 5-mile circular tour (aboard a quaint light-railway train) provides visitors with an insight into the area's development from a glacier, to lake, fen and finally a peat bog. The driver's commentary touches on the use of peat (the Irish call it 'turf') as a fuel in both the domestic hearth and the nearby power station.

159

Day trips by rail

Visitors to Dublin have an easy way to see some of Ireland's most beautiful and interesting regions.

Railtours Ireland introduced a programme in 1998 with the slogan: 'Do a big chunk of Ireland in one day.'

The service now operates from Monday to Saturday all year. Most of the rail tours are combined with coach travel and driver/guides. You may book one day and travel the next.

Get yourself to the appropriate Dublin terminal – Heuston or Connolly — checking in 20 minutes before departure (usually 0720 or 0730), then you can relax and enjoy yourself for the rest of the day. Most trips return to Dublin by 2130 or 2200.

Tours include a couple of half-day trips. Prices range from £19 for a half-day trip to Avoca – the setting of TV's *Ballykissangel* (*see page 150*) – to £89 for a two-day visit to Connemara.

Itineraries

Railtours Ireland, 58 Lower Gardiner Street, Dublin 1. Tel: 856 0045 for details.

Cork, Blarney Castle and Lakes of Killarney: You leave the train at Cork and have a choice; either kiss the Blarney Stone at Blarney Castle, or visit the Queenstown Story Heritage Centre in Cork's restored railway station and Cork Harbour's transatlantic terminal where the *Titanic* made its last port of call.

For ultra-spectacular scenery, take the **Ring of Kerry** tour and see mountain and sea views. This one can be extended with an overnight option in Killarney.

Another spectacular is the **Cliffs of Moher** tour, on the wild Atlantic coast. You get there

by coach from Galway City, with views of Galway Bay. After seeing the weird and fascinating 'moonscape' of the Burren, you go through Co Clare to Bunratty Castle, catching the train home from Limerick.

On the two-day **Connemara Capital** tour, you visit Galway City, cross the Shannon at Athlone and travel through the Connemara mountains and other memorable landscapes to Clifden, the capital. Next day you travel south to the country's Irish-speaking *Gaeltacht* area.

See Northern Ireland on the **Hills of Donegal and Causeway Coast** tour. You change trains at Belfast, taking a quick look at the city, then see the wildly scenic Causeway Coast from the train to Derry. A coach trip through the valleys and glens of Donegal includes a visit to W B Yeats's grave at Drumcliffe. *This tour departs only on Saturdays.*

Two historic cities, Kilkenny and Waterford, are visited in the leisurely **East Coast** tour. The return journey goes through the Vale of Avoca. This tour departs from Heuston and returns to Connolly.

Galway, Connemara and the town of Westport on Clew Bay are featured in a trip across the midlands to the West of Ireland.

A half-day tour to the site of the Battle of the Boyne (1690), Newgrange, the passage tomb that pre-dates the Egyptian pyramids, and other archaeological sites (*see pages 148–149*), is packed with interest – and there's shopping at Slane village, too. The train goes by fishing villages on the east coast.

Religion

The striking ruins of ancient monastic settlements, often in spectacular locations, such as those at Glendalough in the Wicklow Mountains, or Clonmacnoise on the River Shannon, are a reminder of the important role Christianity has played in the lives of the Irish people over the past 1500 years or so.

Religion, especially Roman Catholicism, continues to be a dominant force today. Freedom of conscience and the free profession and practice of religion is guaranteed to all citizens under the Irish Constitution.

The 1991 census found that 91.6 per cent of Ireland's population were Roman Catholics, 2.5 per cent were Church of Ireland (Anglican), 0.4 per cent Presbyterians, 0.1 per cent Methodists and less than 0.1 per cent Jewish. About 3 per cent belonged to other religious groupings or had no specific religious beliefs.

The Roman Catholic Church

The Catholic Church has four ecclesiastical provinces, each with its own archbishop: Armagh, Dublin, Cashel and Tuam, covering the north, east, south and west of the country, respectively. Each province consists of a number of dioceses, of which there are 27 in all. The Archbishop of Armagh is the Primate of All Ireland and is normally a Cardinal. The present diocesan structure has remained basically the same since the 12th century and does not conform to modern political divisions.

The combined Catholic population of the Republic and Northern Ireland is about 3.9 million. The rate of religious practice among Irish Catholics is one of the highest in the world. There are about 20,000 men and women in various religious orders of priests, brothers and nuns.

The Catholic Church is closely involved in the provision of education and health services and co-operates with State agencies in many areas, such as education and welfare. More than 4500 Irish missionaries work in 85 countries throughout Africa, Asia, Central and South America and Oceania.

The Church of Ireland

The Church of Ireland is a Protestant Episcopal Church, autonomous within the worldwide Anglican Communion, and organised into 12 dioceses. The Archbishop of Armagh is the Primate of All Ireland and the only other Archbishopric is Dublin. Chief legislative power lies with the General Synod, consisting of the archbishops, bishops, 216 representatives of the clergy and 432 representatives of the laity. The clerical and lay representatives are elected every three years.

The Church of Ireland is actively involved in education and social services and the total membership of the church is around 380,000, of whom 75 per cent live in Northern Ireland.

The Presbyterian Church

The Presbyterian Church is a Protestant Church of the Reformed tradition and a member of the World Alliance of Reformed Churches. The Reformed tradition lays strong emphasis on the authority of the Scriptures in the life of the Christian.

The 562 congregations are grouped into 21 districts called Presbyteries. Ministers and elders represent their congregations at Presbytery and at the five regional Synods. The Moderator, who presides at the annual General Assembly, is elected as the principal public representative of the Presbyterian Church in Ireland for a one-year period only.

Various commissions, boards and committees are responsible for the detailed work in specialised areas on an ongoing basis. Women have been ordained to the ministry of the Presbyterian Church in Ireland since the 1950s. There are approximately 300,000 Presbyterians in Ireland, some 12,000 of whom live in the Republic, where they are a small but significant minority.

Lifestyles

Shopping, eating, children and nightlife in Dublin

Shopping

Quality is the hallmark of Ireland's irresistible products – crystal, textiles, fine china, knitwear, whiskey, liqueurs, farmhouse cheeses, smoked salmon. It is enduring and it doesn't come cheap, so if you're looking for something really special, prepare to dig deep.

On the other hand, there's plenty of affordable choices in some gift and souvenir shops if you want to lower your sights a little. Almost every major attraction has its gift shop offering a variety of goods – tea cloths, table mats, T-shirts, key rings, ornaments and masses of novelty and fun items. There tends to be a shamrock-with-everything aspect, but the recipients will at least remember where the gift came from.

For the friend who has everything (and preferably lives alone), how about an Irish pipe with a booklet on how to play it and some traditional Irish tunes?

Dublin has some fine department stores selling such items as Irish pewterware mugs in exquisite designs, linen which will last for ever and distinctively crafted jewellery with a Celtic influence.

Spend time in **Clery's** in O'Connell Street and **Arnott's** in Henry Street. Both have dedicated Irish shops within the store. Wander around **Brown Thomas** in Grafton Street, where everything from a velvet scarf to a cocktail shaker has a classy look.

Beautiful Irish crafts, including Waterford crystal, bone china, jewellery and textiles attract visitors to the **House of Ireland** in Nassau Street near Trinity College. Those who couldn't make up their minds in the shop have a second chance as they leave for home from Dublin Airport – the company has a branch in the departure hall.

Many people head for pedestrianised Grafton Street first. This is the exciting core of the city's shopping experience, and it's handy for other main streets. One of the joys of shopping in Dublin compared with most European capitals is that it's compact and manageable while offering a good variety of shops, boutiques and other retail outlets.

For high fashion, Grafton Street and its environs certainly won't let you down, and for the mass market there's **Marks & Spencer's**

MARKS & SPENCER

shops, places to eat, fashions for the young set (and others), fancy goods — there's something on the three floors to appeal to everyone. On the ground floor is an enormous **Dunne's**, a good-value store with 100 branches throughout the country. Clothes for the whole family, food, drink and much more can be bought here. Take a look at **The Donegal Shop** on the top floor with its fine selection of handwoven tweed jackets for men and women, homespun tweed caps and hats, traditional handknitted polo sweaters and handloomed Aran cardigans and sweaters in 100 per cent wool.

Even in the dead of winter the flower stalls are piled high with glorious blooms, and there's nearly always a busker somewhere, playing the fiddle expertly or singing his heart out. It's a place with a joyous atmosphere, and whatever intentions you start out with you'll find yourself in a what-the-hell spending mood.

At the southern end of Grafton Street, **St Stephen's Green Shopping Centre** stands like a multi-decked cruise ship. Specialist

Another of Dublin's prestigious shopping centres is the **Powerscourt Townhouse** in William Street South. Converted from a Georgian mansion in the 1980s, it still has the original mahogany staircase. Antiques and art works, clothing, jewellery and other goods provide pleasurable browsing and buying, and there are places to relax over coffee or tea.

Kennedy and McSharry, in Nassau Street, has been a noted menswear shop for more than a century, and a few doors away at **Kevin and Howlien** you can buy a length of tweed or ready-made jackets for men and women.

The Jervis Centre, off Henry Street, is useful for fashion shopping. For general shopping away from the city centre, malls can be found in most of Dublin's suburbs.

Indoor market

People with an eye for the unusual and those who are natural born collectors should make a weekend bee-line for **Mother Redcap's Market**. Although it's all indoors, the booths line little streets. All sorts of bric-à-brac, antiques and collectables and general flea-market discoveries are on sale. There are old photographs, good knitwear, furniture, mats, nails and screws, electrical items, paintings, gadgets and heaven knows what. Mother Redcap's is in an old brick building in Back Lane, across Cornmarket from St Audoen's Church. The

entrance is fairly inconspicuous. If you can't find it, you'll know you're getting warm when you hear the music (*Fri, Sat and Sun 1000–1730*).

Temple Bar

Developed from 18th- and 19th-century warehouses and other buildings which fell into decay, Temple Bar has been transformed into Dublin's arty-crafty, slightly bohemian, cultural centre. It has tiny boutiques, galleries, and a good sprinkling of craft and one-of-a-kind shops.

This is the place to look for the off-beat, the unusual. Clothes have a distinctly individual character. Dozens of little restaurants, cafés and pubs, dimly lit, with shadowy entrances, are dotted among the narrow cobbled pedestrianised streets.

Temple Bar night-spots buzz with activity until the small hours, street art takes on curious forms, such as vintage tractors piled one on top of another, open-air theatre performances and street events take place in summer, and live music is never far away. The Irish Film Centre is based in Temple Bar.

If you're looking for contemporary Irish art – and there's some impressive talent about – you should stroll around **Arthouse**, a multimedia arts centre in Curved Street. It costs nothing to look, and you can buy if you want to, choosing from some 4000 works, or perhaps commissioning an artist. *Tel: 605 6800. Mon–Fri 0900–1830, Sat 1000–1800. Temple Bar Information Centre, 18 Eustace Street, Temple Bar, Dublin 2. Tel: 671 5717.*

Shop opening hours in Dublin's centre are generally Mon–Sat 0900–1800 (to 2000 on Thur). In the suburbs Friday is the usual late opening night. Some of the major city centre stores now open for six hours on a Sunday, usually between 1200 and 1800.

Out of town

Tourists used to go to Avoca, an easy hour's drive south of Dublin, to see **Avoca Handweavers** and possibly buy their lovely tweed suits, coats and jackets. They still do, but another reason is that the small village in wooded, hilly countryside is now famous as the setting of the TV soap *Ballykissangel* (*see page 150*). As well as gorgeous clothes and accessories, Avoca Handweavers sells crafts and gifts and has a restaurant. If you can't see what you want here, call at the company's outlet at Kilmacanogue, near Bray, on the way back to Dublin.

VAT refunds

If you're from a non-European Union country be sure to ask for a special VAT receipt when you make purchases, so you can claim a VAT (Value Added Tax) refund on your purchases in Ireland. The receipts should be stamped at the airport customs and a cash refund made.

" *I live in County Clare. I draw back my curtains every morning and see County Clare. Now why would I want a picture of County Clare?* **"**

Woman to man selling paintings in Mother Redcap's Market

Eating out

The cuisines of a dozen nations can be sampled in and around Dublin, but Ireland can hold its head high among any of these. The fertile land, washed only too often with soft rain, is the source of good, wholesome produce. Emerald grass is converted into succulent lamb and beef. Dairy cattle give creamy milk which is used to make excellent butter and cheeses.

Salmon grow big and tender in clear, fast-flowing rivers. Smoked salmon is a treat the world over, and nobody does it better than the Irish. Good catches of trout and perch are made. The sea yields a generous harvest of haddock, whiting, mackerel, plaice and skate, and several species of shellfish, including crab, lobster, scallops and oysters. Dublin Bay prawns are a delicacy in any language.

Pheasant, partridge, venison, hare and wild duck appear on many Dublin menus. The humble rabbit, enjoyed casseroled or in a pie in Irish homes, rarely makes it to the city's dining establishments, which is a pity considering its low cholesterol, tender flesh and subtle flavour.

Roast duck, cooked crisply, plump chickens which have foraged around farmyard and field, pork from rootling pigs and the finest hams, smoked to perfection or left 'green' – these farm-reared meats, cooked without embellishment, have given the cuisine of modern Ireland a high reputation.

What a pleasure it is, too, to sit down to a breakfast of bacon rashers that aren't watery, eggs with rich orange yolks, juicy mushrooms with a good, earthy flavour and savoury meaty sausages.

The Irish pride themselves on their breads. You may come across a few Dublin pubs – the Turk's Head in Parliament Street is one – where they serve neat slices of four or five different breads with their soup. Probably the best known outside Ireland is soda bread, a yeastless dough in which buttermilk or sour milk, rolled oats and bicarbonate of soda are used. The dough is shaped into a round and a deep cross cut into it, so that when it's baked you get four plump quarters. It takes little time to prepare, needs no proving and bakes in about 45 minutes, so it can be cooked in time for breakfast – it really does need to be eaten fresh.

Boxty is another speciality – bread made with potatoes, some mashed, some grated, and flour. Very filling, very tasty. It's served warm, in the form of well-risen rounds, spread with butter.

Potatoes, of course, have traditionally been the mainstay of the Irish diet, and Irish cooks have some special ways with them. They jazz up mashed potatoes by adding chopped spring onions (scallions) to them and call it champ. Ideally, the spring onions should be simmered in a little milk before mixing them, with the milk, into the potatoes. Sometimes fresh chopped chives, uncooked, are used instead of spring onions.

Potato soup, perfectly seasoned, is another dish in which the Irish excel. Potato and leek soup, and potato and parsley soup, are hearty and sustaining choices and it is extremely rare to come across any soup in a pub or restaurant that is less than perfect.

171

They may not be exactly what the doctor ordered, but if you have a heavy sightseeing session ahead of you, potato cakes with your meal will prevent flagging. They're made from a mixture of mashed potatoes and finely-chopped cooked cabbage and a powdering of flour, all blended together over a low heat in a little boiled milk with bacon fat added. And that's not all! The mixture is moulded into cakes and fried in more bacon fat.

Dublin has a number of extremely talented chefs, some of whom have worked in prestigious kitchens around the world. As the city's palate becomes increasingly sophisticated, a few of the old favourites, like boiled ham and cabbage, potato dumplings and Irish stew, are getting more difficult to find away from the rural areas.

A good Irish stew is worth tracking down. It usually comes with nice chunky carrots and possibly pearl barley. Purists will tell you that if it has anything but layers of neck of lamb, onions and potatoes with herbs, stock and seasoning, it isn't authentic Irish stew. But who's going to complain about a few carrots as long as it's cooked long and slowly to thicken up the juices?

One delectable dish that appears on many restaurant menus is beef in Guinness, or any other Irish stout. It's a simple casserole of cubed steak, onions, mushrooms and stout, and according to one Dublin chef, a little soft brown sugar works wonders for the flavour.

People who eat fish but no meat will fare very well in Dublin. They may find a delicious scallop and mushroom pie in which scallops and haddock harmonise happily.

As vegetarianism grows in influence, more restaurateurs are recognising the market. Dublin may not be the most vegetarian-conscious capital in Europe, but efforts are being made in some catering establishments. Juice, in South Great Georges Street, is one that is ahead of the field, serving interesting dishes that won't break the bank. There's a juice bar, and wines, too.

Some general restaurants are responding to the trend, including one or two 'proper' veggie dishes that are exciting enough to entice non-vegetarians to give it a whirl.

Dublin and the area can offer just about any foreign cuisine – American, Belgian, Cajun, Chinese, French, Greek, Greek-Cypriot, Indian, Italian, Japanese, Malaysian, Mexican, Nepalese, Pakistani, Russian, Spanish and Thai.

“ *Eat fish, live longer. Eat oysters, love longer.* **”**

Advertising slogan of the seafood kitchen at Johnny Fox's pub at Glencullen in the Dublin Mountains

Drinking

Ireland is very civilised about its drinking. Whiskey has been a comfort and joy for centuries (*see pages 144–145*). Guinness is the great national thirst-quencher, though you don't have to be thirsty to drink it. Other stouts, like Murphy's and Beamish, have their following. Kilkenny is one of the tastier ales, a bit like a tawny stout in the way it holds its creamy head.

Dublin with children

Although very much a city for grown-ups, Dublin has plenty to amuse and stimulate younger visitors in or near the city.

Talk to the animals

Dublin Zoo, in Phoenix Park (*see page 115*), has enough to occupy a child's attention for hours: a jolly train ride, a pet-care section, play areas for little ones, a discovery

centre and all the animals. There's a World of Primates, with chimpanzees, spider monkeys and other species on islands in a large lake, and a section of cold-climate creatures – polar bears, arctic foxes and snowy owls. Many rare animals and birds can be seen. *Tel: 677 1425. Mon–Sat 0930–1800, Sun 1030–1800. Earlier closing in winter. Admission: £££; family ticket available.*

Waxing lyrical

Small children will be enchanted to find themselves amid familiar characters in the World of Fairytales and Fantasy at the National Wax Museum (*see page 29*). Older ones will enjoy shuddering at ghastly encounters in the Chamber of Horrors and meeting such stars as Madonna and

Elvis in the flesh – well, almost. *Granby Row, Parnell Square, Dublin 1. Tel: 872 6340. Mon–Sat 1000–1730, Sun 1200–1730. Admission: ££; concessions.*

Where Dublin began

Sail a stormy sea as the Norsemen did 1000 years ago and land in the Viking settlement of Dyflin. Here you are invited into a Viking home to hear from the occupant what everyday life was like. Although the time travel aspect of Dublin's Viking Adventure has general interest, it has particular appeal for children, especially those who will enjoy banter with the Norse sea-captain. There's a cleverly-presented cross-section of Dublin through the ages, with Viking Dyflin at the base. A museum and gift shop complete the experience (*see page 91*). *Essex Street West, Temple Bar, Dublin 8. Tel: 679 6040. Tue–Sat 1000–1630. Admission: ££; concessions.*

Arts at the Ark

The Ark is a cultural centre for children which holds workshops, concerts, art and other exhibitions and presents performances in its own theatre, all designed to appeal to 4 to 14-year-olds. You'll need to book and to check on what programmes are scheduled during your visit (*see page 88*). *Eustace Street, opposite Temple Bar Information Centre, Temple Bar. Tel: 670 7788. Tue–Fri 0930–1600.*

Paddle your own...

With all equipment supplied, no previous experience necessary and qualified instructors in attendance, you can enjoy Dublin Bay by kayak. A mini-bus picks you up at the Suffolk Street tourist centre, returning 3 hours later. Pre-booking is essential. *Adventure Activities, 5 Tritonville Avenue, Sandymount, Dublin 4. Tel: 668 8047. Mon 1630, Thur 1000, Fri 1900. Family ticket available.*

Playing trains

Set among superb models of Dublin landmarks, the Fry Model Railway is in a fascinating museum in the grounds of Malahide Castle. Model locomotives and coaches were made by a former railway engineer (*see pages 136–137*). *Tel: 846 3779. Open all year, times vary. Admission: £.*

Rock and burgers

Rock 'n' roll memorabilia, including guitars signed by rock stars and U2's original drum kit, can be seen at **Captain America's**, where they serve more than a dozen types of burger. *44 Grafton Street, Dublin 2. Tel: 671 5266. Daily noon–midnight.*

After dark

Ireland is a nation of performers. You can book a ticket for an orchestral concert or see something classical at the theatre. Or you can be chatting with the locals in a pub and suddenly there's a party. Someone has brought his fiddle along, someone else joins in with a bodhran – a small goatskin drum – or a tin whistle, feet begin to tap and a session has begun.

Not all pub entertainment is impromptu. You can rely on a lot of places to have something good organised nightly – possibly Rhythm and Blues or Country and Western,

but far more likely to be Irish. Whether a few friends strike up spontaneously or whether it's a well-rehearsed group or a big name, you're unlikely to be bored.

Where they started

U2 cut their rock teeth at such venues as the **Baggot Inn**, more or less straight from school, and recorded their first album, *Boy*, at the Windmill Lane Studio in the early 1980s. The walls there have become a shrine to U2 and other Dublin groups, with 'free art' and messages to stars by fans from all over the world.

Chris de Burgh, whose world tours are a sell-out, busked among the burgers at **Captain America's** in Grafton Street when he was a Trinity College student.

A corner of the **Gresham Hotel** in O'Connell Street reverberated to The Chieftains' lusty voices before they released their first album in 1964. Bob Geldof formed the Boomtown Rats in Dublin more than 20 years ago in **Bewley's**, Grafton Street. The Dubliners got together in a back bar at **O'Donaghue's** in

Merrion Row in the early 1960s. Sinéad O'Connor, who made her first record in 1982 when she was 14, augmented her income as a teenage waitress in the **Bad Ass Café** in Dublin's Crown Alley.

The music you will hear in the intimacy of a Dublin pub or hotel bar may be played by embryonic successors to U2 or Geldof.

The clubs

One of Dublin's liveliest nightclubs is **The Kitchen** in the Clarence Hotel at Wellington Quay. It is owned by U2, who have resurrected the 1920s hotel.

Most of the nightclubs are in Leeson Street, off St Stephen's Green. The **Burlington Hotel** in Upper Leeson Street features a classy Irish cabaret. The snappy dressers among the young set dance the night away at **The PoD** in Harcourt Street.

For dancing to music from the 1960s, 70s and 80s, try the Leftbank Bar in Anglesea Street, Temple Bar. La Med, in Essex Street, Temple Bar, has a jazz bar. Irish music sessions and dancing nights are held at Lanigan's Pub at the Clifton Court Hotel, O'Connell's Bridge, where turf fires and candlelight set the mood.

The brother of rock singer Bono owns the **Tosca Restaurant** in Suffolk Street. Visiting musicians go there and it's popular with actors. Bono himself, so they say, is sometimes seen in **The Dockers Pub** at Sir John Rogerson's Quay, near the

Windmill Lane Studio. Sing-alongs are held here, and also at the **Brazen Head**, where Irish music nights are a regular feature.

Out-of-town spots that Dubliners love include the **Abbey Tavern** at Howth, where great Irish entertainment is staged, and **Johnny Fox's Pub** at Glencullen. They have 'hooley' nights with ballad singers and the Fox's Irish Dancing Troupe. Another is **Polly Hops**, a venerable inn and restaurant at Newcastle, southwest of Dublin. As well as impromptu sessions, there are party nights with singing, dancing and story-telling.

To see a selection of good pubs in a short time, take the **Musical Pub Crawl**, which starts from the Oliver St John Gogarty pub in Fleet Street, Temple Bar and visits four other pubs.

177

After a surfeit of Irish, how about a boogie night at the Break for the Border American bar, nightclub and restaurant in Lower Stephen Street?

Performing arts

Dublin takes great pride in its performing arts. The **Abbey Theatre**, incorporating the smaller Peacock Theatre, in Lower Abbey Square, is noted for its Irish classics and (in the Peacock) the work of new

writers. Contemporary works are staged at the **Gate Theatre**, Parnell Square. Performances of general and family appeal are presented at the **Gaiety Theatre**, South King Street, where dance, drama, opera and musicals take place. The **Olympia Theatre** in Dame Street stages music events and family entertainment.

Venues for experimental theatre include the Andrews Lane Theatre, the Tivoli in Francis Street and the Project Arts Centre, East Essex Street.

Classical music is performed at the National Concert Hall, and the occasional gig is held there.

For a mobile form of drama, join the **Trapeze Theatre Company** in a nocturnal 'Walk Macabre'. Murder, the supernatural and other horrors are enacted at some of the city's scenes of violence and evil.

Ghosts and ghouls

Other after-dark spine-chillers are the **Dublin Ghost Bus Tour**, which takes you to scenes of body-snatching, hauntings and **Dracula's Dublin** connections and, in the comfort of the Legal Eagle Tavern, you are introduced to the superstitions of a traditional Irish wake.

The **Zosimus Experience** is another ghoulish tour, on foot through the cobblestones of medieval Dublin.

After that, how about a good laugh? Comedy theatre is increasingly enlivening the entertainment scene and the **Tivoli Theatre** is one venue. Irish and international stand-up comedians dispense hilarity at **Murphy's Laughter Lounge** at Eden Quay, O'Connell Bridge.

Dublin's many cinemas in the centre and suburbs offer cheaper seats before 1700. The giant-screen IMAX Experience and the nine-screen Virgin Cinema are both in the Parnell Centre, Parnell Street – an ultra-modern entertainment centre with family attractions, themed bars and restaurants.

Fancy a flutter? There's greyhound racing on Mon, Tue and Fri evenings at Harold's Cross (in Rathmines, $1^1/_2$ miles south of the city centre).

Keep an eye on the major daily newspapers for details of what's on. The fortnightly *Hot Press* gives the low-down on the music scene. Regulars on the Dublin calendar are the Film Festival in March, the three-day Guinness Blues Festival in late July and the two-week Dublin Theatre Festival in October.

Tickets and information on most events, theatres, shows and tours are available from the Ticket Desk, Dublin Tourism Centre, Suffolk Street, Dublin 2. *For ticket reservations by credit card tel: 605 7777.*

" *Once I asked a Dublin policeman to tell me the exact time ... and he replied at once without the ghost of a smile that the exact time was between two and three.* "

Honor Tracy, journalist and author

179

Practical
information

PRACTICAL INFORMATION

Practical information

Airport

Dublin's only airport is 6 miles north of the city centre. The terminal building is at last being updated and enlarged, with new duty-free shopping zones and roomier catering facilities. There are desks operated by major car rental companies as well as a post office,

There is no rail service between airport and city. Taxis are in abundance though relatively expensive, but *ask first*).

Airlink is an express coach service run by Dublin Bus (*tel: 873 4222*). It runs between the airport, the central bus station and Heuston railway station. The fares are £2.50 to the city centre and £3 to Heuston Station. Buses run every 20–30 minutes from the airport Mon–Sat 0640–2300, Sun 0710–2300. From the city centre they run Mon–Sat 0705–2225, Sun 0735–2230, and from Heuston Station Mon–Sat 0820–2030, Sun 0805–2215.

Climate

Ireland's weather is notoriously capricious, but the good news is that Dublin lies within the country's driest area. However, that doesn't mean you can leave the raincoat and umbrella behind. Similarly, although the climate is generally temperate, with average temperatures rarely falling below O°C (32°F) or climbing above 20°C (68°F), you'd be wise to pack a sweater even in the summertime. All in all, it's a good climate for sightseeing on foot at most times.

bureau de change and a tourist information centre covering the whole of Ireland, as well as Dublin, and offering an accommodation reservations service.

Aer Rianta, the Irish airports authority which manages the airport, operates an information centre (*tel: 704 4222*), and flight information is available by dialling 1550 200200.

Currency

Ireland's currency unit is the punt, or Irish pound (IR) and 100 pence = IR£1. Coins are 1p, 2p, 5p, 10p, 20p, 50p and £1. 1p and 2p coins are copper, 20p coins are gold-coloured and the remainder are silver. Notes are £5 (yellow/brown), £10 (green), £20 (purple) and £50 (blue). Major credit cards are widely accepted. As always when travelling abroad, travellers' cheques are the safest way to carry substantial sums of money. Banks and bureaux de change are the best places to cash travellers' cheques or change money – you may be charged too much anywhere else.

Customs regulations

Unless a proposal to abolish duty-free allowances in the European Union is implemented, citizens of Britain and other European countries travelling to and from the Republic of Ireland have the same duty-free privileges as travellers from elsewhere in the world.

The present allowances are: 200 cigarettes or 100 cigarillos or 50 cigars or 250g of tobacco; two litres of fortified or sparkling wine or one litre of spirits; 60ml perfume; 250ml toilet water. There are restrictions on importing meat and meat products.

EU citizens over the age of 18 are allowed to import 800 cigarettes, 45 litres of wine and 55 litres of beer provided duty was paid at the point of purchase. From the age of 16, non-EU citizens may import goods on which tax has been paid up to the value of £142. Up to 16 the allowance is £73.

Disabled travellers

Facilities are getting better for visitors with disabilities, and many tourist sights throughout Ireland now have access for wheelchairs, but it would be wise to check by telephone before setting off. Major car-parks have spaces set aside for vehicles carrying disabled persons, and an orange badge scheme allows disabled drivers to park without charge.

An access guide to accommodation, restaurants and amenities is published by the **National Rehabilitation Board** *24–25 Clyde Road, Ballsbridge, Dublin 2,* which also offers advice to visitors with disabilities. Wheelchairs may be hired from the **Irish Wheelchair Association** *24 Blackheath Drive, Dublin 3; tel: 833 5366.*

Buses in Dublin are not equipped to accommodate disabled passengers, and many train stations are difficult. However, **Iarnród Éireann** *Connolly Station, Dublin 1; tel: 836 3333,* will arrange for disabled travellers to be met at the station and accompanied to the train if notified beforehand. They will also remove seats for those intending to remain in their wheelchairs during their journey. Dining cars on InterCity trains now have easy access areas. The InterCity Guide for Mobility Impaired Passengers, available at any DART or railway station details the easiest access at stations nationwide.

Electricity

Power throughout the Republic is 220V AC (50 cycles). Plugs are the same as those in the UK, with three square pins.

Entry formalities

British citizens born in the UK and travelling from Britain do not need a passport to enter Ireland, but it would be wise to take one since Irish immigration officers are now asking arriving passengers, especially at airports, to show some form of identification. This follows a recent increase in illegal immigrants using Britain as a 'back door' to Ireland. A passport is also convincing identification when renting a car or cashing travellers' cheques.

Citizens of other EU countries, the United States, Canada, Australia, New Zealand and South Africa must have a valid passport, but do not need a visa to enter Ireland. Travellers with a Hong Kong Certificate of Identity will need an entry visa. Applications for visas should be made through the Irish Embassy or Consulate in your country or direct applications may be made to: *The Consular Section, Department of Foreign Affairs, 72–76 St Stephen's Green, Dublin 2; tel: 478 0822; fax 668 6518.*

Health

EU residents can claim free medical treatment in Ireland, but should obtain a Form E111 from their national social security department or nearest post office before leaving home. You will need to make sure that the doctor you consult in Ireland is registered with the Health Board Panel and you should show the doctor the Form E111 and some form of identification before the consultation or treatment begins. Visitors from non-EU countries should have adequate medical and accident insurance.

General medical care facilities are available at **Grafton Street Medical Centre** *Dublin 2; tel: 671 2122*; or **Mercer's Medical Centre** *Stephen Street Lower, Dublin 2; tel: 402 2300.* Dental treatment: **Grafton Street Dental Practice** *Grafton Medical Centre; tel: 6719200*; or **Molesworth Clinic** *2 Molesworth Place, Dublin 2; tel: 661 5544.*

A wide range of medical supplies and contraceptives is available over the counter at pharmacies, but many medicines are available only on prescription. The following pharmacies have extended opening times: **Corrigans** *80 Malahide Road, Dublin 3; tel: 833 8803. Open Mon–Sat 0900–2200, Sun 1030–1900, bank holidays 1000–1900.* **O'Connell's Late Night Pharmacies** *Grafton Street, Dublin 2; tel: 679 0467; Mon–Sat 0830–2030, Sun 1100–1800; O'Connell Street, Dublin 1; tel: 873 0427; Mon–Sat 0830–2200, Sun 1000–2200.*

Telephone 999 or 112 if you need an ambulance. There are 24-hour accident and emergency departments at **Adelaide and Meath Hospital** *Tallaght, Dublin 2; tel: 414 3500; or Beaumont Hospital, Beaumont Road, Dublin 9; tel: 809 2714.*

Information

The main source of tourist information is **Dublin Tourism Centre** *Suffolk Street, Dublin 2; tel: 605 7799 (information), 605 7777 (reservations). Mon and Wed–Sat 0900–1730, Tue 0930–1730, closed 25–26 Dec and 1 Jan.* The office is very user-friendly and has a wide range of leaflets, brochures, maps – many of them free – covering other parts of Ireland, as well as Dublin. Accommodation reservations and ticket bookings are also available. *Tel: 1550 112 233 for 24-hour visitor information.*

Other tourist offices are in the arrivals hall: **Dublin Airport** *open daily 0800–2200, closed 25–26 Dec and 1 Jan*; **Dun Laoghaire Ferry Terminal** *daily 0800–1300, closed 25–26 Dec and 1 Jan*; **The Square, Town Centre, Tallaght** *daily 0800–1300, closed bank holidays.*

Dublin Tourism's newspaper-style guide is packed with information on things to do and see, where to eat, drink, dance, sing, etc. For the latest gossip on gigs and groups buy a copy of *Hot Press*, available at most newsagents. A full range of information and an accommodation reservations service are available on the Dublin Tourism website: *www.visit.ie/dublin.* Travel advisers can deal with direct inquiries and accommodation reservations e-mailed to *reservations@dublintourism.ie.*

Insurance

Even if you are covered for medical costs under the EU reciprocal arrangements, it makes sense to take out travel insurance when visiting Dublin – or indeed, anywhere else. Your policy should include cover against third-party liability, lost baggage and cash, travel delays and trip cancellation. If you have to pay for medical treatment, remember to keep all receipts to present with your claim.

Opening times

Banks
Mon–Fri 1000–1600, with late opening to 1700 Thur. ATM facilities are available at many branches in the city.

Most post offices
Mon–Fri 0930–1730, Sat 0900–1300. The General Post Office, O'Connell Street: *Mon–Sat 0800–2000, Sun and bank holidays 1030–1830.*

Shops
Generally Mon–Fri 0930–1730, with late opening at major shops in the city centre Thur to 2000 and Sat to 1800. Some department stores in the city centre open for four hours on Sun, usually 1200–1600.

Pubs
Most pubs serve Mon–Sat 1030–2330, Sun 1230–1400 and 1600–2300. All pubs close Good Friday and Christmas Day.

Public holidays

New Year's Day (1 Jan), St. Patrick's Day (17 Mar), Good Friday, Easter Monday, May Day (first Mon in May), June Holiday (first Mon in June), August Holiday (first Mon in Aug), October Holiday (last Mon in Oct), Christmas Day (25 Dec), St Stephen's Day (26 Dec).

Reading

James Joyce is almost certainly the first name to spring into most people's minds when they think of Dublin and books. *Ulysses*, of course, is the classic, but it is hard going (if you fancy a real challenge for your holiday read, try Joyce's last book, *Finnegan's Wake*). Joyce took a more conventional look at the pre-World War I city in *Dubliners*, and in *A Portrait of the Artist as a Young Man* you can detect the stirrings that led to *Ulysses*.

Others who have included Dublin's fair (and sometimes dark and brooding) city in their fiction are Brendan Behan *Borstal Boy*, Maeve Binchy *Dublin 4*, Dermot Bolger *Night Shift*, J P Donleavy *The Ginger Man*, Roddy Doyle *The Commitments, Paddy Clarke Ha Ha Ha* and Liam O'Flaherty *Insurrection*.

For history buffs there are the three volumes of Robert Kee's *The Green Flag* or A *Concise History of Ireland* by Máire and Conor Cruise O'Brien. If you're the kind of person who cares about the origin of street names and what building stood where in the past, Douglas Bennett's *Encyclopaedia of Dublin* should keep you happy for hours.

Safety and security

Although violent street crime is rare, it's best to take sensible precautions and stay out of Dublin's less savoury areas and darker side-streets. Hotel and tourist office staff will gladly tell you which parts to avoid. Pickpockets may be active in crowded shopping malls, so don't carry passports or large amounts of cash with you. Valuables and luggage should be kept out of sight when you park the car which should, of course, be locked.

Emergency telephone numbers for the police ('Garda' in Irish), fire and ambulance services are 999 or 112.

Telephones

Public telephones are either coin- or card-operated and calls cost a minimum of 20p. Telephone cards can be bought at newsagents and post offices. The area code for Dublin is 01, but the prefix should only be used from outside Co Dublin. Numbers prefixed 1800 are free. Cheap-rate calls operate Mon–Fri 1800–0800 and all day Sat–Sun and public holidays.

To make an international call dial 00 then the appropriate country code. Some commonly used codes are Australia 61; Germany 49; Japan 81; South Africa 27; UK 44; USA 971. To call Dublin from abroad dial 353 for Ireland after the international access code then 1 for Dublin.

If you need operator asistance to make a call dial 10 for Ireland and the UK and 114 for an international call. Directory inquiries: 1190 for Ireland, 1197 for the UK and 1198 for international inquries.

Time

Ireland is in the same time zone as Britain (Greenwich Mean Time): five hours ahead of Eastern Standard Time in the USA, an hour behind western Europe, ten hours behind Sydney. Clocks go forward one hour for daylight saving in the summer.

Toilets

Shopping malls and centres and some big stores are the most likely places to find clean and serviceable public toilets, as are most tourist locations. There are ladies' (Mna in Irish) and gents' (Fir) facilities near the Anna Livia Fountain on O'Connell Street. Pub managers are not keen on people using their facilities without at least buying a drink.

Index

Discover Dublin

Editorial, design and production credits

Project management: Dial House Publishing Services
Series editor: Christopher Catling
Copy editor: Posy Gosling
Proof-reader: Susie Whimster

Series and cover design: Trickett & Webb Limited
Cover artwork: Wenham Arts
Text layout: Wenham Arts
Map work: RJS Associates

Repro and image setting: Z2 Repro, Thetford, Norfolk, UK
Printed and bound by: Artes Graficas ELKAR S. Coop., Bilbao, Spain

We would like to thank Larry Dunmire for the photographs used in this book, to whom the copyright in the photograph belongs, with the exception of the following:

Dublin's Viking Adventure: page 90
Paul Murphy: pages 100 and 101
National Museum of Ireland: page 113
Image Select International: pages 150, 155 and 157
J Allan Cash: page 151
AA Photo Library: page 154
Spectrum: page 159

The authors would like to thank the following people and organisations for assistance given during the researching of this guide: Aer Lingus; Louise Bisoni; British Airports Authority; London Stansted Airport; Dan Dooley Car Hire; John Lahiffe and the Irish Tourist Board, London; Catherine McClusky and Dublin Tourism; Terry McGovern.

Picture research: Deborah Emeny; Image Select International